This Book is the property of

The Milestone School

Issued to:—

NAME	DATE	MASTER'S INITIALS	GRADE

Combined Science 1
Teachers' guide

Safety Note

The wearing of eye shields should be insisted upon in laboratories where there is risk to the eyes and such risks may arise from spills and splashes as well as from explosions.

In experiments which involve the heating of a compound which evolves a gas, care should be taken that there is no risk of a build up of pressure through the blocking of a tube.

From Safety in Science Laboratories (*D.E.S. publication*)

Combined Science 1
Teachers' guide

Geoff Green
Oulder Hill School, Rochdale
Ken Petford
Alan Short
David Walker
Ashton-under-Lyne Grammar School

John Murray   London

Set in IBM 10 on 11 pt Press Roman with 11 pt
Univers Bold
Printed and bound in Great Britain by
Morrison & Gibb Ltd, London and Edinburgh
Illustrated by Denys Baker

0 7195 3263 9

Contents

Preface

Combined Science 1 is the first of two books each of which covers at least one year's work of an integrated science course for pupils starting secondary education. The books comprise a definite course rather than a collection of topics although flexibility of sequence is possible.

With integration of disciplines we appreciate that during some part of the work almost all teachers will be on unfamiliar ground; an attempt has, therefore, been made to give as much help as possible in this teachers' guide.

The experimental material has been tested with pupils of a wide range of ability and the instructions are such that the minimum of help should be required. However, we hope that the book will prove to be more than a collection of recipes and will have an intrinsic interest of its own. The factual content of the course, and the scientific approach it is hoped it will foster, make it a very suitable springboard for more advanced courses of integrated science or the separate disciplines of biology, chemistry, and physics.

We took part in the trials for Nuffield Combined Science and freely acknowledge our considerable debt to the organizers of that scheme for both stimulation and apparatus which has been made available through their pioneering. We are also very grateful to Mr D. Marchant who read the manuscript for the publishers and made many helpful criticisms, and to Mr A. Bhatt and Mr P. Butler, two senior pupils at Ashton-under-Lyne Grammar School, who helped with the preliminary preparation of drawings.

Thanks are due to the following for permission to use their photographs in this book: figures 1.3 and 7.2, C. Fogg; figure 2.4, Peter J. Hoare.

1975

G. Green
S. K. C. Petford
A. J. Short
D. L. Walker

1 Our world

The photographs and questions which begin this chapter are intended to stimulate the pupil's interest from the beginning. Satisfactory answers to these questions (1 to 10) are given below for the teacher's information. Pupils will probably not be able to answer them at this stage but should come across the answers as they work through the book.

Q1 They are fingerprints and the line patterns on them are different.
Q2 They help by neutralizing some of the acid in the stomach.
Q3 The numbers represent inches of mercury.
Q4 The weather.
Q5 A plugged worm burrow.
Q6 Because it is filled with a gas which is lighter than air (hydrogen or helium).
Q7 Table salt is produced from this rock salt by purification.
Q8 Annual rings each representing a year's growth.
Q9 The surface tension of the water prevents it from sinking.
Q10 Mammals.

Exhibition of materials

Before the first lesson as wide a selection as possible of different materials should be set out in the laboratory in such a way as to allow the pupils to look round freely. The choice of materials is left to the teacher but it is desirable that as many as possible of the items listed below be included.

biological specimens and	industrial methylated spirits
laboratory animals	local biological material
charcoal	metallic ores
copper(II) sulphate crystals	naphthalene (pure and impure)
crude oil and associated products	rock salt
different leaves	rock specimens
fossils	various bones

Suitable materials and/or wallcharts which will be found useful either here or later may be obtained from the organizations listed on page 78.

The purpose of the exhibition is to stimulate interest and to form a basis for the later work on classification.

Odd one out

A Bicycle — only one with two wheels
B Rugby ball — not spherical like the others
C Sparrow — the only bird listed, the others are mammals
D Plastic — it is non-metallic and all the others are metals
E Fir — a coniferous tree, the rest are deciduous

The pupils may suggest alternative and equally valid answers to those given above.

Dividing into two groups

A Oak, ash — trees (plants)
Cow, horse — animals

B Sugar, salt — edible
Sulphur, iron — non-edible

C Dandelion, daisy — flowering plants
Fern, moss — non-flowering plants

D Kiwi, emu — flightless birds
Parrot, eagle — birds which fly

E Whale, monkey — mammals
Lizard, snake — reptiles

Again alternative answers may be equally valid.

Q11 Animals and vegetables are or were living things.

Living things

Q12 The most notable features of living things are:
reproduction (see Chapter 10)
growth (see Chapter 11)
breathing (respiration) (see Chapter 8)
feeding

Movement, which many pupils will suggest, is more characteristic of animals than of plants.

Experiment 1.1 Finding the living things in leaf litter

Each group requires:
 forceps
 hand lens
 large quantity (sackfull) of old leaf litter
 newspaper (1 sheet)
 plastic boxes, petri dishes, or pill boxes (3)

Alternative method

If leaf litter is not readily available, soil can be used. The apparatus
shown in figure 1.1 (Tullgren's apparatus), which can easily be made,
provides a useful method of extracting animals from soil. For a class of
about thirty pupils, three or four of these, set up well before the
lesson, will be needed.

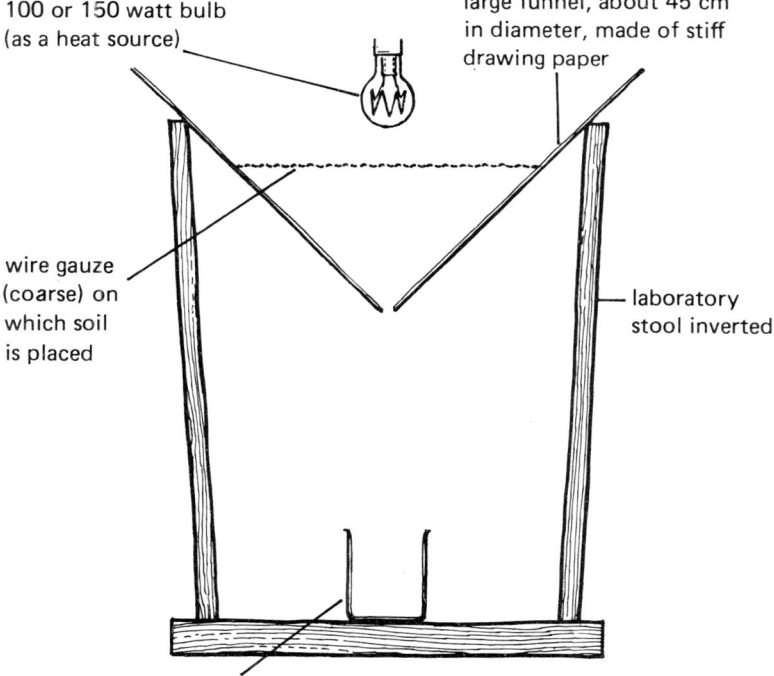

100 or 150 watt bulb
(as a heat source)

large funnel, about 45 cm
in diameter, made of stiff
drawing paper

wire gauze
(coarse) on
which soil
is placed

laboratory
stool inverted

beaker to collect specimens driven from soil by heat

Figure 1.1 Tullgren's apparatus.

Classifying living things

Living things can be divided into *plants* and *animals*. But these two
groups are very big and it is not easy to make statements which can be
applied either to all animals or to all plants. For this reason, the plant
and animal kingdoms are divided into smaller groups called *phyla*
(singular - *phylum*). All things that belong to the same phylum have
several features in common. For example, man, cow, and dog all belong
to the phylum *vertebrates* because, among other things, they all have a
skeleton of bone-like substance and a backbone. The main phyla of the
plant and animal kingdoms are listed in tables 1.1 and 1.2.

Classification of animals into phyla

Vertebrates
Animals with backbones (see table 1.4)

Echinoderms
Marine. Internal skeleton. Usually have five
arms. These may be joined together however.
e.g. starfish, sea cucumber

Molluscs
Soft body with one coiled shell or two
uncoiled. Large muscle-like foot. e.g. slug,
snail, oyster

Arthropods
Hard jointed external skeleton. Paired jointed
legs (see table 1.3)

ANIMAL
KINGDOM

Annelids
Worm-like with rounded bodies made up of
segments. e.g. earthworm

Platyhelminths
Flat worm-like bodies. Not segmented. e.g.
tapeworm, fluke

Coelenterates
Cylindrical bodies with central mouth. Often
have tentacles. e.g. *Hydra*, jellyfish, sea anemone

Protozoa
Body not divided into cells. e.g. *Amoeba*

Table 1.1

Classification of plants into phyla

Flowering plants
Green plants. Well-developed root, stem, and leaf system. Great variation in size. Some small and soft-stemmed; others trees with woody stems. Produce flowers and seeds. e.g. buttercup, sycamore

Conifers
Green plants. Well-developed root, stem, and leaf system. Leaves often needle-like. Seeds borne in cones. e.g. fir trees

Horsetails and ferns
Green plants with well-developed leaf and root system. Contain vascular tissue. Reproduce by means of spores

PLANT KINGDOM

Liverworts and mosses
Usually small green plants. Plant body grows flat in a seaweed-like fashion. Some have short stems with leaf-like structures attached. They are attached to surfaces by fibrous root-like structures. Live on land in damp places

Fungi
Plant body lacking root, stem, and leaves. Do not contain chlorophyll. Most are made up of thread-like filaments which may be compacted into quite large structures. e.g. moulds, toadstools

Algae
Plant body lacking root, stem, and leaves. Contain chlorophyll. Some have additional red or brown pigment. Single-celled or multicellular with a flattened often ribbon-like body. Sometimes large plants. Mainly aquatic. e.g. *Spirogyra*, seaweed

Table 1.2

Even within a phylum there are still many plants or animals which are quite different from each other. Therefore, each phylum is divided into smaller groups called *classes*. The main classes of arthropods and vertebrates are given in tables 1.3 and 1.4, while figure 1.2 shows the main features of the four classes of arthropods. Many of the animals found in leaf litter or soil belong to the phylum arthropods.

Main classes of the phylum Arthropods

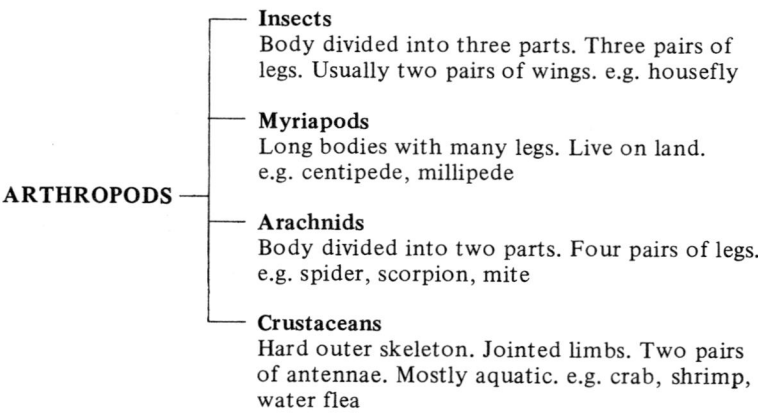

ARTHROPODS

Insects
Body divided into three parts. Three pairs of legs. Usually two pairs of wings. e.g. housefly

Myriapods
Long bodies with many legs. Live on land. e.g. centipede, millipede

Arachnids
Body divided into two parts. Four pairs of legs. e.g. spider, scorpion, mite

Crustaceans
Hard outer skeleton. Jointed limbs. Two pairs of antennae. Mostly aquatic. e.g. crab, shrimp, water flea

Table 1.3

Main classes of the phylum Vertebrates

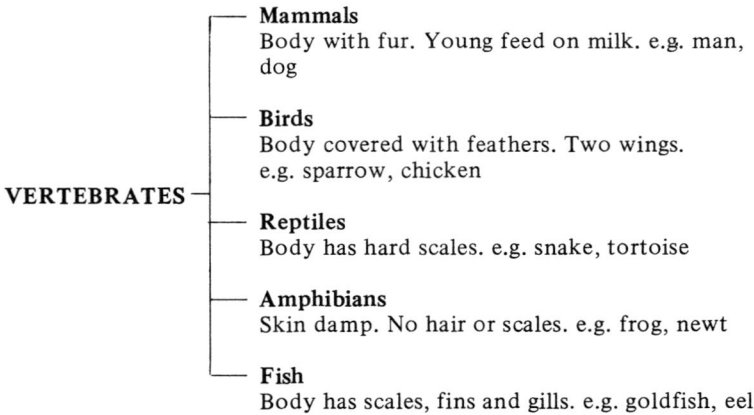

VERTEBRATES

Mammals
Body with fur. Young feed on milk. e.g. man, dog

Birds
Body covered with feathers. Two wings. e.g. sparrow, chicken

Reptiles
Body has hard scales. e.g. snake, tortoise

Amphibians
Skin damp. No hair or scales. e.g. frog, newt

Fish
Body has scales, fins and gills. e.g. goldfish, eel

Table 1.4

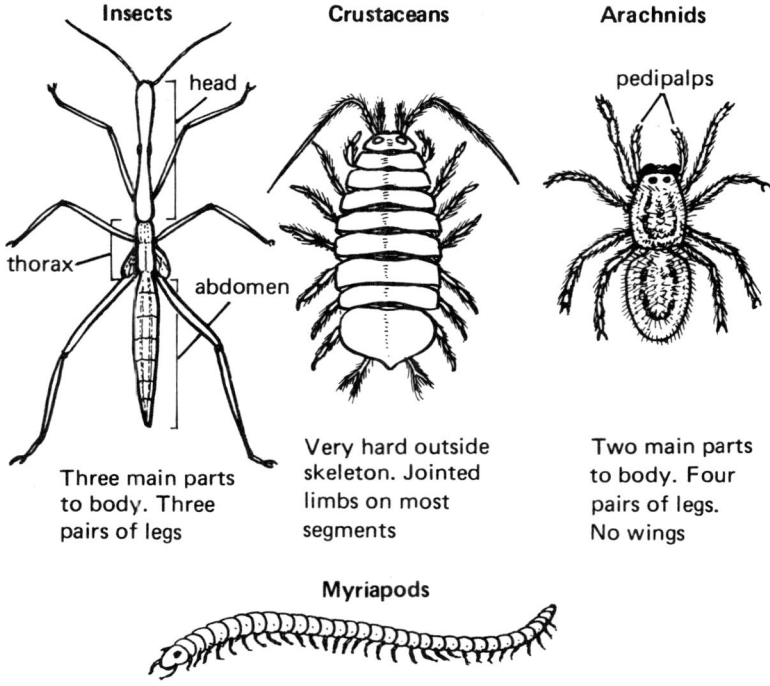

Insects

head

thorax

abdomen

Three main parts
to body. Three
pairs of legs

Crustaceans

Very hard outside
skeleton. Jointed
limbs on most
segments

Arachnids

pedipalps

Two main parts
to body. Four
pairs of legs.
No wings

Myriapods

Body divided into many *similar* segments.
Similar pairs of limbs attached to most body segments

Figure 1.2 The main features of the four classes of arthropods.

Classes are further divided into smaller groups, each known as a
genus, which in turn are made up of a number of different *species*. All
members of a species are the same kind of plant or animal. Man is a
single species of animal and the common daisy a single species of plant

Thus the main groups into which living things are divided, in order
of importance, are: kingdom, phylum, class, genus, species.

Q13 Mammals.
Q14 They all suckle their young and have hair on some parts of the
body (very little in the case of the whale, dolphin, and porpoise).

Experiment 1.2   Identifying leaves of common trees

Each group requires:
    ruler marked in cm
    selection of leaves from those listed in the key (see figure 1.3)

Figure 1.3 Leaves for Experiment 1.2: **a** oak; **b** silver birch; **c** privet; **d** mountain ash; **e** horse chestnut; **f** sycamore; **g** ash.

Making your own keys

The example below illustrates the method of making up a key. A key for the same animals using the same features could be made up in a different way or other characteristics could have been chosen. It is the experience of the authors that children need a great deal of help in making their first key, but soon improve with practice.

A simple key for farm animals was arrived at as follows:

Animals to be keyed: duck, hen, cow, horse, pig, dog.

1 Select features which show suitable clear differences and record the differences in tabular form (table 1.5).

Animal	Legs	Feet webbed or not webbed	Feet hooved or not hooved	Has horns or does not have horns	Size
Duck	2	webbed	not hooved	no horns	small
Hen	2	not webbed	not hooved	no horns	small
Cow	4	not webbed	hooved	has horns	large
Horse	4	not webbed	hooved	no horns	large
Pig	4	not webbed	hooved	no horns	medium
Dog	4	not webbed	not hooved	no horns	medium

Table 1.5

2 Convert this table into a branching diagram to highlight the differences and number each point of branching (table 1.6).

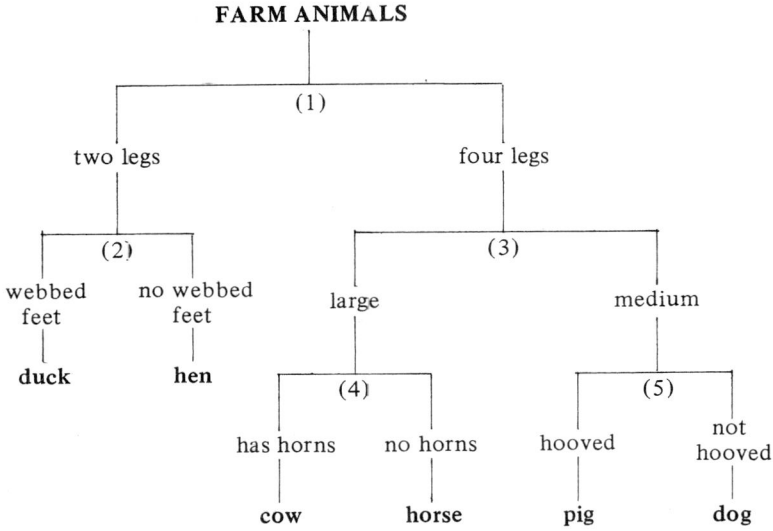

Table 1.6

3 Write pairs of questions in the form shown below.

A key for farm animals

1	Animal has two legs	Go to 2
	Animal has four legs	Go to 3
2	Animal has webbed feet	*Duck*
	Animal does not have webbed feet	*Hen*
3	Animal is large	Go to 4
	Animal is medium sized	Go to 5
4	Animal has horns	*Cow*
	Animal is without horns	*Horse*
5	Feet of animal are hooved	*Pig*
	Feet of animal are not hooved	*Dog*

Experiment 1.3   Looking at fingerprints

Each group requires:
cottonwool
fingerprint ink (obtainable from laboratory suppliers)
glass sheet (microscope slide would be reasonably satisfactory)
hand lens
plain white paper (1 sheet)
spatula or wooden splint
methylated spirits

Q17   The left-hand one has a loop pattern and the right-hand one a whorl.

Experiment 1.4   How many seeds are there in a gorse pod?

Each group requires:
gorse pods (2)

Pea pods could be used where gorse pods are not available. However, the wastage of foodstuff in this way is not to be encouraged and gorse pods or lupin pods should be used if possible. SAFETY: Many common pods and their seeds are poisonous, e.g. laburnum.

This section attempts to illustrate the fact that the simple arithmetic mean is not always useful.

Q21   Size 5.
Q22   Thirty-four girls.
Q23   Sizes 3 and 6½ are least common.

Making your own bar chart

Materials required:
statistics frame
supply of graph paper

Note. Some pupils may not have come across the term 'mass' but the authors feel they should be encouraged to use it from the start of the course to avoid confusion later. See the note in Experiment 5.7.

As an additional or alternative approach to producing a normal distribution curve, the following procedure might be adopted.
    Determine the height in centimetres of each pupil in the class. Choose suitable narrow height ranges and select one pupil from each height range. Draw a straight line on the floor and have the selected children line up, shoulder to shoulder, in order of height along this line.

The remaining members of the class should then line up close behind the pupil in the line representing the height range in which their own height falls. Then draw a chalk line on the floor just touching the heels of the last person in each file. When the pupils move away a curve approaching a normal distribution curve should be clearly visible.

If, by this method, a normal distribution curve is not obtained, then a good opportunity arises to stress the need for a large and thereby representative sample being taken before valid conclusions may be drawn. This, indeed, needs to be pointed out frequently throughout this work.

It may be possible and worth while to carry out this procedure using all the pupils in a particular year to see if a better curve results.

Other things to do

1 (*a*) The largest mammal is the blue whale. One slightly in excess of 33 metres in length and 136.4 tonnes in mass has been recorded. (*b*) The largest land mammal is the bull African elephant. One approximately 4 metres high at the shoulder and 11 tonnes in mass has been recorded. (*c*) The tallest mammal is the giraffe. With neck erect some have been found to be almost 6 metres tall. (*d*) The tallest known race of Man is the Tutsi of Africa with an average height for men of 185 centimetres.

3 (*a*) *Mammals.* Some part of the body has hair, young are fed on milk, diaphragm is used in respiration, lower jaw is made up of a single pair of bones. Three bones, the malleus, incus, and stapes, connect the ear drum to the middle ear. Only the left systemic arch of the blood system is present. Large brain.

(*b*) *Birds.* Body covered with feathers making possible a high constant body temperature. Fore limbs modified to form wings. They have a lot of reptile features also, e.g. presence of horny scales on legs and feet. The bones are light and strong, many containing air sacs — outgrowths from the lungs. A keel is present on the breastbone for the attachment of large flight muscles. Sense of sight very acute therefore optic lobes of the brain very large. Have a beak made of keratin but lack teeth.

(*c*) *Fishes.* Aquatic and cold blooded. Use the oxygen dissolved in the water for breathing. The breathing organs are gills. Movement is by powerful tail muscles and by paired and median fins. The heart is two-chambered. Most authorities would now divide fish into four distinct classes rather than group them as a single class.

2 Wonderful worms

This chapter contains the first series of experiments that pupils will have been called upon to carry out, and the importance of a clear record should be stressed. Whilst not wanting to suggest the traditional 'Experiment, Apparatus, Method, Results, Conclusion', the need for possible reference-back later on should be pointed out. A clear fully labelled diagram is very useful in reducing the amount of writing necessary. Discussion of the value and setting out of results could be found fruitful at this point.

Experiment 2.1   Investigating earth mounds

The ground being investigated ought to include, if possible, areas of cut grass, gravel, soil, paved areas, and so forth.

Worm casts may be found on any or all of such sites but most will probably be found on the cut grass.

Q1 Earthworms (many, though not necessarily all, children will know this already).
Q2 Worm casts.
Q3 Probably on the cut grass.

Experiment 2.2   What are worm casts made of?

Each group requires:
dissecting needle   hand lens
newspaper on which to spread out the worm casts

The following materials may be found in worm casts: soil, grass, pebbles, moss, and pieces of brick, roots, glass, and so on.

Q4 Answers will vary. No 'correct' answer can be given.

Experiment 2.3   How much soil do earthworms move?

Each group requires:
containers suitable for holding worm casts   pegs (4)
metre rule   string (4 m)
access to: balance capable of weighing to an accuracy of 1 g

If there are very few worm casts on the chosen sites then a larger area should be pegged out.

Q10 In wet weather the water content of the casts will be higher, so increasing their mass.

Q11 The simplest way would be to dry the worm casts each time before weighing.

Experiment 2.4　What do worms look like?

Each group requires:
dissecting needle	newspaper (1 sheet)
hand lens	worm

A good supply of worms can often be found in compost heaps or in other places where the soil is damp.

This experiment is designed to encourage observation rather than the identification of different species of worm.

Q12 Basically round, but flattened possibly at the posterior end.

Q13 Yes, but it may not be visible.

Q14 No.

Q15 No, but it has short bristle-like structures (chaetae) which some pupils may detect.

Other features which may be noticed include: anus, male apertures, colour difference between dorsal and ventral surfaces, segments, ventral blood vessel (see figure 2.1).

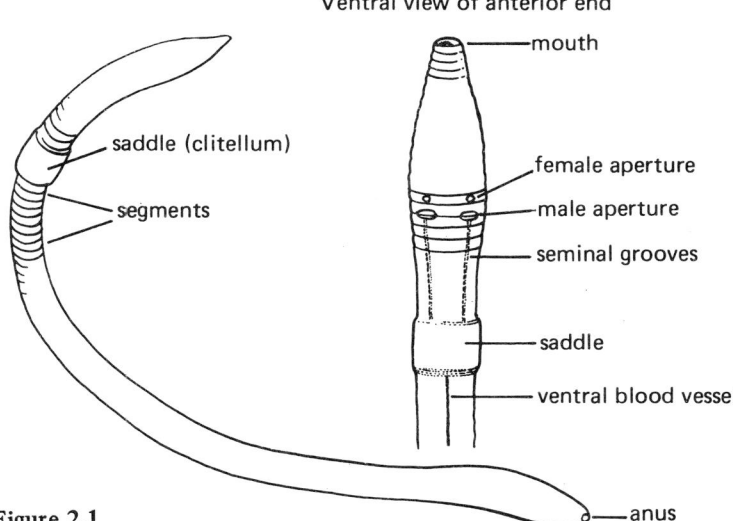

Ventral view of anterior end

Figure 2.1

Q16 No.

Q17 Moist (probably).

Q18 About ten different kinds of earthworm are commonly found in Britain. The most common is the small·*Allolobophora caliginosa* (about 5 cm long). Of the larger worms, if they are over 15 cm they are probably either *Lumbricus terrestris* (the common earthworm) or *Allolobophora longa* (the long worm). These are, of course, much easier for the pupils to handle.

Experiment 2.5   How do earthworms move?

Each group requires:
    smooth-surfaced paper (1 sheet)
    worm

Q19 Detailed study of worm movement is very complex. Pupils may, however, notice that the anterior end first becomes longer and thinner while the posterior end grips the surface. The posterior end is then brought up so that the worm becomes shorter and fatter.

Q20 A scratching noise is heard as the worm moves.

Q21 Bristle-like structures.

Q22 The bristles (chaetae) moving over the paper.

Q23 They provide a better grip.

One way to test this answer is to compare the movement of the worm on both rough and smooth (e.g. glass) surfaces which are tilted to the same angle.

Experiment 2.6   Do earthworms respond to light?

Each group requires:
    coloured materials for putting in front of the light source
    newspaper (1 sheet)
    torch or other source of light
    worm
access to:
    room with blackout

Q24 – Q26 In general, worms move away from bright lights.

Q27 Worms are much less sensitive to coloured lights and least of all to red.

Q28 Individual worms may not respond in this way and so the class results are important (similar things are different!).

Experiment 2.7   Do earthworms respond to touch?

Each group requires:
    blades of grass (1 or 2)
    drinking straw
    newspaper (1 sheet)
    pencil
    worm

Q29 The anterior end.

Results with other objects may vary widely but should prove interesting.

Q30 The worms were sensitive to mechanical vibrations which is important for survival in their natural habitat.

This can lead to some interesting open-ended and imaginative experimentation.

Experiment 2.8   Setting up a wormery

Each group requires:
    active worms (about 6)
    moist soil
    wormery — pattern and suggested dimensions are shown below.

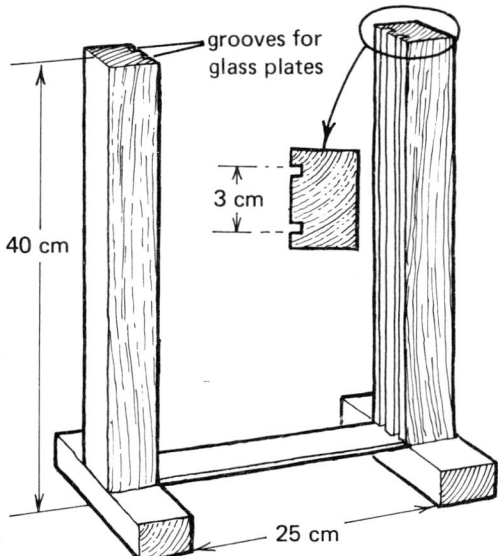

Figure 2.2 A suitable form of wormery.

The purpose of this experiment is to show the formation of burrows and to find out something about them (size, shape, etc.). Glass jars serve as simple but less effective wormeries.

Q31 Burrows.
Q32 Usually the anterior end.
Q33 Probably not.

Experiment 2.9   Do earthworms turn over the soil?

Each group requires:
    active worms (about 6)
    leaves of various kinds
    moist sand
    moist soil
    wormery

It is essential that the soil in the wormery be kept moist. It should be looked at once each week.

Q34 The alternating layers make it possible to see any mixing.
Q35 Probably, yes.
Q36 Some leaves may have been dragged into the burrows.

Experiment 2.10   Looking for worm burrows

Pupils should be directed to areas where plugged burrows are plentiful.

Q37 Pupils should feel slight resistance to the pull indicating that the leaves have been drawn into the burrow.
Q38 The entrance to the burrow.
Q39 Most likely not.

Experiment 2.11   Do earthworms prefer certain kinds of leaves for plugging their burrows?

Figure 2.3 shows one method of answering this question, which has been used successfully. For this method each group of pupils would need:

    leaves of various kinds
    plant pot, 15 cm diameter

The arrangement of leaves suggested ensures that each leaf has an equal chance of being selected. With a little encouragement or prompting the pupils will suggest this arrangement.

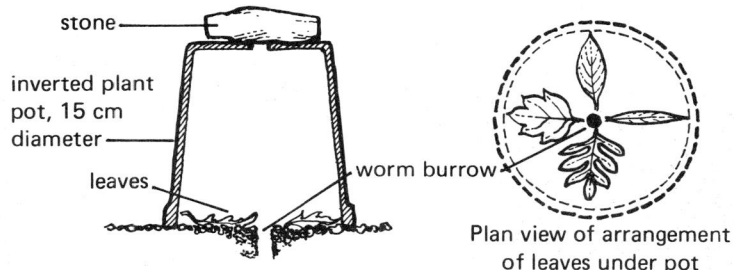

Plan view of arrangement
of leaves under pot

Figure 2.3

When choosing the leaves, mint leaves and pine needles are of interest because of their smell. Very large leaves, such as horse chestnut and sycamore, are best avoided.

The pots should be inspected daily. If a burrow is found to be plugged the procedure can then be varied as follows:

a the choice of material noted and the pot removed; *or*
b the material noted and removed and the experiment then reset exactly as before. In this case the observations continue for a fixed period, e.g. a week.

Conclusions from a single experiment cannot be considered valid. Therefore, the results of the whole class or, better, the whole year, should be combined.

Q40 No definite answer can be given here as it depends upon the materials used. However, the class or year results should be considered together before any conclusion is reached.

Q41 Useful discussion can arise about the reasons for the choice. These may include sense of smell, shape, colour, and so on. Discussion may lead to further experiments which pupils can do at home.

Q42 It is not really known why worms plug their burrows but several suggestions are likely to be put forward, such as protection, camouflage, prevention of flooding.

Q43 Yes, because decaying vegetable matter will produce more humus thus increasing the food content of the soil.

The soil from worm casts contains particles of ideal size for plant growth. The spaces between the particles hold enough water and also allow enough air space for the plant roots.

'Bright ideas' (hypotheses)

Figure 2.4

Show the pupils the photograph of the bird and milk bottle after they have made their own suggestions.

The actual reasons for the observations which the pupils are asked to investigate are given below. Pupils may suggest others which, within the limits of their knowledge at this stage, seem equally valid.

a Shoot systems grow towards the greater light on the window side *(phototropism)*.

b The gas at the centre of the inner (blue) cone is not burning and thus the temperature is below the ignition point of the match head.

c Heat travels more quickly along the copper rod than it does along the iron one as copper is a better conductor of heat than iron.

d The ash from the bonfire contains mineral salts which stimulate growth of the grass.

3 Making things pure

Experiment 3.1   Looking at rock salt

Each group requires:
  hand lens
  pestle and mortar
  watchglass or sheet of paper
  rock salt
  table salt

If rock salt is not available, pure sodium chloride mixed with grit or powdered carbon provides a satisfactory alternative.

Q1 No, there are different coloured impurities.
Q2 'Washing with water' is a likely suggestion. This should be tried and it should be pointed out that, although some of the impurities are clearly removed in this way, many are, equally clearly, left behind.

Experiment 3.2   Making salt disappear

Each group requires:
  spatula
  test-tube, 100 x 16 mm
  pure sodium chloride

Experiment 3.3   Making the salt reappear

Each group requires:
  asbestos mat
  Bunsen burner
  hand lens
  microscope slide
  teat pipette
  tongs or wooden clothes peg
  salt solution from Experiment 3.2
access to:
  infra-red lamp on stand

Q4 Pure salt.
Q5 This question is aimed at provoking class discussion as a lead-in to Experiment 3.4.

Experiment 3.4   Purifying rock salt

Each group requires:
  beaker, 100 cm^3
  Bunsen burner
  evaporating basin
  filter funnel and filter paper
  gauze
  glass stirring rod
  hand lens
  pestle and mortar
  retort stand and ring, or filter funnel stand
  tripod
  crushed rock salt

Q6 Sand (and other insoluble impurities which may be present).
Q7 Pure salt (assuming all impurities are insoluble in water).
Q8 Yes, they should be similar.

Experiment 3.5   Does water dissolve all things?

Each group requires:
  Bunsen burner
  filter funnel and filter paper
  hard-glass test-tube, 100 x 16 mm
  retort stand and ring, or filter funnel stand
  tongs or wooden clothes peg
  naphthalene

Q9 No, it is insoluble.
Q10 No.

Experiment 3.6   Purifying naphthalene

Each group requires:
  beaker, 100 cm^3
  Buchner funnel and flask
  Bunsen burner
  dry test-tubes, 100 x 16 mm (2)
  filter paper to fit Buchner funnel
  gauze
  glass stirring rod
  spatula
  tripod
  ethanol (industrial methylated spirits)
  impure naphthalene (see note below)

Impure naphthalene from an industrial source may not be very suitable for this experiment as the impurities may be soluble in ethanol if they are organic compounds. Pure naphthalene mixed with a small amount of powdered carbon is a suitable alternative.

It should be stressed that ethanol must be heated in a water bath and not directly by a Bunsen flame. In this way the risk of the vapour catching fire is reduced. A water bath should always be used for heating when practicable.

The use of rapid filtration under reduced pressure, using a Buchner funnel, is introduced here solely to illustrate the technique which is an important one to the organic chemist. Conventional filtration at ordinary pressure will be equally effective but a filter funnel with as short a stem as possible is preferable to minimize the risk of crystallization occurring in the funnel.

Q11 On the filter paper; crystalline.
Q12 White.
Q13 More pure; those impurities insoluble in ethanol have been removed.
Q14 Moth balls.

Experiment 3.7 Another way of purifying naphthalene

Each group requires:
beaker *with lip,* 250 cm^3
Bunsen burner
gauze
retort stand and clamp
round-bottomed flask, 500 cm^3
tripod
impure naphthalene as in Experiment 3.6

WARNING. There is a slight risk of fire with this experiment if too high a flame is used or the beaker does not have a lip.

Q15 Naphthalene.

Experiment 3.8 Filtering ink

Each group requires:
filter funnel and filter paper
test-tubes, 100 x 16 mm (2)
black (or blue) ink

Q16 No (it will be stained black or blue).
Q17 Yes, it should be.
Q18 No. Refer back to salt solution. A solute cannot be separated from a solution by filtering.

Experiment 3.9   Evaporating ink

Each group requires:
anti-bumping granules or pieces of unglazed porcelain
beaker, 250 cm^3
Bunsen burner
conical flask, 250 cm^3, fitted with bung and delivery tube as in the
    students' book diagram
gauze
test-tube
tripod
black or blue ink diluted with an equal volume of water

The purpose of the anti-bumping granules is to promote even boiling
and prevent a sudden surge of ink passing over without separating. They
probably work by enabling small bubbles to be formed on their porous
surfaces so inhibiting the formation of large bubbles which cause
'boiling with bumping'.

The attention of pupils should be drawn to the dangers of
'sucking back' if the end of the delivery tube reaches below the
surface of the liquid collected in the test-tube and heating is stopped.

Q19   Colourless.
Q20   To cool it so that the vapour condenses.
Q21   Ink is *not* a single substance; therefore it is not pure.
Q22   Add the distillate to the residue.

Demonstration experiment 3A   Distillation of ink

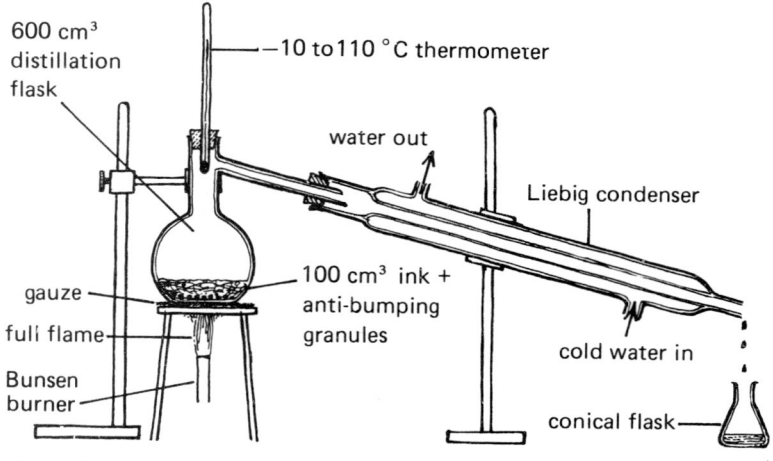

Figure 3.1

Set up the apparatus as shown in figure 3.1, making sure that:

a all stoppers fit tightly;
b water is flowing through the condenser in the right direction;
c the bulb of the thermometer is opposite the side-arm of the distillation flask.

Heat the distillation flask so as just to keep the ink boiling. (If necessary a few pieces of wooden splint may be added to minimize frothing.) When a liquid starts to collect in the receiver (conical flask), read the thermometer. Continue heating until the distillation flask is almost dry.

Q24 Colourless.
Q25 100 °C. (However, depending upon the accuracy of the thermometer and fluctuations in atmospheric pressure, the boiling point may be up to about 2 °C above or below the 'correct' value.)
Q26 Water – it boils at 100 °C.
Q27 Cooling so that the steam condenses back to water.
Q28 Black (or blue) residue of the solute. There is no evidence to say whether or not it is a pure substance.

If one is available, the pupils may usefully be shown a film or film loop at this stage on, say, whisky distillation. It is as well not to complicate matters by showing a film or film loop which includes fractional distillation. This latter subject is considered in Book 2.

Experiment 3.10   Ink spots

Each group requires:
    filter paper   teat pipette or glass rod
    petri dish   test-tube
    black or blue ink (Parker 'Quink Permanent Black' is very good here).

Q29 It has spread out and the colours have separated.
Q30 It is a mixture, that is, it is not a single substance (pure).

Experiment 3.11   Ink strips

Each group requires:
    boiling-tube, 150 x 25 mm   teat pipette (small hole)
    cork to fit boiling-tube   test-tube rack
    drawing pin   black or brown ink
    filter paper, 11 cm diameter   ethanol
access to:
    scissors

Q31 Pupils will probably suggest dissolving it out with water or ethanol. Whilst ethanol will work, acetone gives a better result here.

Experiment 3.12   A chromatogram from grass (or privet)

Each group requires:
   filter funnel
   filter papers (2)
   pestle and mortar
   petri dish
   retort stand and ring, or filter funnel stand
   teat pipette (small hole)
   test-tube, 100 x 16 mm
   acetone
   clean sand
   quantity of freshly cut grass or privet leaves

The chromatogram should show definite green and yellow pigments.
The green dye is *chlorophyll* and the yellow one *xanthophyll.* A third
pigment, *carotene,* is present but does not usually show by this method.
   If available, a film or film loop on the extraction of chlorophyll
could usefully be shown at this point.

   Q32 The green matter is not a pure (single) substance.

Experiment 3.13   Boiling point of a liquid

Each group requires:
   Bunsen burner
   retort stand and clamp
   side-arm test-tube with stopper
   thermometer, −10 to 110 °C
   anti-bumping granules
   distilled water

Q33   100 °C (subject to the accuracy of the pupils' thermometer).

Experiment 3.14   Is the boiling point affected by dissolved substances?

Each group requires:
   Bunsen burner
   retort stand and clamp
   side-arm test-tube with stopper
   thermometers, −10 to 110 °C (2)
   anti-bumping granules
   salt

Q34 (*a*) It would be higher because dissolved solutes raise the
boiling point of a liquid. (*b*) It would be unchanged because only

the solvent and not the solute evaporates.

Q35 The boiling point of impure water would be higher.

Experiment 3.15   Melting point of a solid

Each group requires:
boiling-tube (hard-glass), 150 x 25 mm
Bunsen burner
fine capillary tube, 8 cm long (1 or 2)
retort stand and clamp
rubber band or thin slice of rubber tubing of suitable bore
thermometer, −10 to 110 °C
wire stirrer
solid naphthalene

The melting point of naphthalene is 80 °C.

Other things to do

1 Separation is possible by mixing the sugar and sand in warm water, when the sugar will dissolve. The sand may be removed as the residue on filtering. By evaporating the filtrate, sugar solution, the sugar may be obtained.

2 Trichloroethene, petroleum ether, propanone, and benzene find many uses in the textile and dry cleaning industries for the removal of waxes and fats, etc. Chloroform is a solvent for polystyrene.

3 Distillation is carried out in the petroleum and salt industries, and in the manufacture of whisky.

4 Sweet and sour

It is strongly recommended that, at the start of the first lesson on this topic, each pupil be given an acid drop (such as an acid 'Spangle') to suck. Pupils should then be asked to describe the taste. Answers such as sour, bitter, or acid are likely.

In the following experiments great care should be taken to prevent contamination of solutions by the use of different glass rods or teat pipettes. Alternatively, the rod or pipette should be washed thoroughly for each different solution.

Experiment 4.1   Investigating sourness

Each group requires:
> drinking straws cut into short lengths for taking samples to taste
> test-tube rack
> test-tubes, 150 x 25 mm labelled, A, B, C, D, and E, containing solutions as follows:
>> A Acid-drop solution made by crushing a few acid drops ('Spangles') and dissolving them in water
>> B Lemon juice, suitably diluted with distilled water (a useful substitute is lemon juice concentrate such as 'Jiffy')
>> C Malt vinegar solution, suitably diluted
>> D Dilute (say 5%) sodium bicarbonate solution
>> E Dilute solution of table sugar (5%)

Note: all dilution and making up of solutions should be done exclusively with distilled water.

Results: A, B, and C all taste sour (acid); D and E do not taste sour (not acid).

Experiment 4.2   Can plant colouring matter show acidity?

Each group requires:
> filter funnel
> filter papers, 9 cm (20)
> pestle and mortar
> teat pipette or glass rod
> coloured flower petals, e.g. rose, delphinium
> raw beetroot, carrot and red cabbage leaves
> solutions A, B, C, D, and E from Experiment 4.1

Extracts of raw beetroot, red cabbage, and carrot can be made by crushing pieces of them with a *little* water in a mortar.

Although pupils should try their own methods, extracts of most flower petals are best prepared in advance as follows. Dried petals are crushed in a mortar with a mixture of equal volumes of ethanol (industrial methylated spirits) and distilled water. The contents of the mortar should then be transferred to a round-bottomed flask and refluxed gently (see figure 4.1) over a boiling water bath until the solid material has gone white (about 20 minutes usually). After the contents have cooled, they are then filtered.

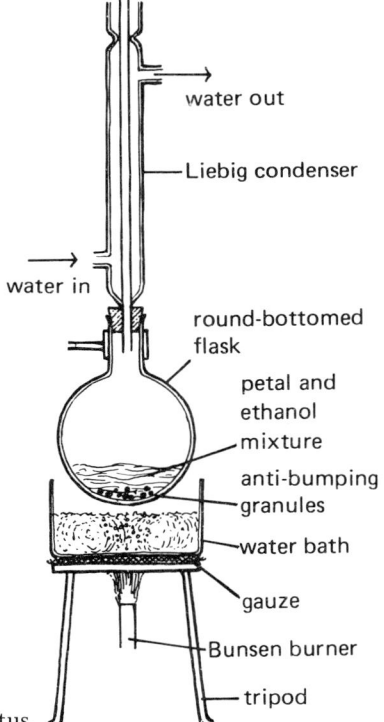

Figure 4.1
Refluxing apparatus.

The following colours should be obtained when the solutions are added to the coloured filter papers:

	With acidic solution (A, B, and C)	With alkaline solution (D)
Beetroot	purple	yellow
Red cabbage	red (pink)	green
Carrot	no change	no change
Flower petals	Depends on flowers used; some may show no colour change	

Q1 Yes, the solutions should group in the same way as using taste (Experiment 4.1). This illustrates that it is not necessary to taste something to detect acidity.

Q2 Most likely not. This will depend upon the extracts used; carrot certainly does not show a colour change and so is probably well worth including to show that all plant pigments are not indicators.

Q3 No, those which do not show a colour change cannot be used as indicators.

Experiment 4.3 Spotting the difference

Each group requires:
>   one of each of the stained filter papers, which showed colour
>   changes from Experiment 4.2
>   teat pipette or glass rod
>   test-tube racks (2)
>   three test-tubes, 150 x 25 mm, as follows:
>>   (a) labelled 'Acid' containing dilute hydrochloric acid solution
>>   (2M)
>>   (b) labelled 'Neutral' containing distilled water
>>   (c) labelled 'Stomach powder solution' containing 10 per cent
>>   sodium bicarbonate solution
>   three test-tubes, 150 x 25 mm, labelled F, G, and H as follows:
>>   F containing distilled water
>>   G containing dilute (M) sulphuric acid
>>   H containing dilute (2M) sodium hydroxide

Q4 If this is done carefully three distinct colours should result, indicating acidic, alkaline, and neutral solutions.

Q5 No. Pupils should gather this from the photographs. For example, lemon juice may be drunk but many other acids cannot.

A range of different concentrations of *weak* acids should be available for the pupils' use.

Q6 Probably not, differences in colour change are not very clear.

Experiment 4.4 Using universal indicator

Each group requires:
>   teat pipette or glass rod
>   test-tube rack
>   universal indicator solution
>   three test-tubes, 100 x 16 mm, labelled A, B, and C containing
>   solutions of various acids, such as:
>   5 per cent boric acid   (pH = 4–6)

5 per cent zinc sulphate (pH = 2)
0.1 M hydrochloric acid (pH = 1)

SAFETY. Pupils should be warned not to test concentrated acids.

Q7 The varying colour changes are a measure of the degree of acidity.

Experiment 4.5   Finding the pH of various substances

Each group requires:
teat pipette or glass rod
universal indicator papers

range of solutions: all except concentrated acids are suitable.
Various dilutions of vinegar (acetic acid) and limewater should be included and several household substances

Experiment 4.6   Removing acidity

Each group requires:
teat pipette or glass rod
test-tubes, 100 x 16 mm (3)
universal indicator solution
solutions for part (a):
    0.1 M hydrochloric acid
    0.1 M sodium hydroxide
solutions for parts (b) and (c):
    acid-drop solution
    sugar solution
    stomach powder solution

SAFETY. It is recommended that the apparatus and solutions from part (a) be cleared away before starting parts (b) and (c) *to prevent the possibility of strong acid solutions being tasted.*

Q8 The addition of alkali results in the neutralization of the acid and the solution finally becomes alkaline. The universal indicator shows this by colour changes.
Q9 Part (b) shows that sugar solution removes the sour taste but does not remove the acidity. Part (c) shows that stomach powder removes both the acid taste and the acidity.

Other things to do

1 Both Tees-side and the Lancashire industrial belt are important areas for acid and alkali production.

5 Measuring things

Q1 12 hours.

Q2 125 metres.

Q3 100 °C approximately.

Q4 60 tonnes (60 000 kg).

Q5 Time, length, temperature, weight.

Q6 Clock, ruler, thermometer, balance.

Experiment 5.1 Making a simple clock

Each group requires:

    cotton thread more than one metre long

    flat metal discs (2p pieces are suitable) (2)

metre rule	retort stand and clamp
pin	small weight (bob)
plasticine	stopwatch

The pin provides a fixed central point for counting the swings. A supply of plasticine should be available for pupils who wish to increase the mass of the bob.

Q7 The pupils' answers will vary: longer length of thread gives slower swing.

Q8 Make the thread (*a*) shorter, (*b*) longer.

Pupils should find that only the length of the thread has any significant effect on the number of swings.

    The bob will pass the pin 30 times in 30 seconds when the length of thread is approximately one metre from the centre of the bob to the clamp on the retort stand.

    Rates of breathing and pulse are suitable for measuring with the simple pendulum clock.

Things to find out

1 Examples: hiring a tennis court; buying washing machine time in a launderette; buying parking time at a parking meter; hiring a man to do a job of work.

2 A candle marked off in equal divisions to represent equal amounts of time.

3 (*a*) The time taken for a point on the Earth's surface facing the centre of the Sun's disc to rotate once on its axis and face that point again (24 hours approximately). (*b*) As (*a*) but replacing the Sun in the definition by a star (23 hours 56 minutes).

Q9 8 cm.
Q10 7 cm.
Q11 6 cm.

Experiment 5.2   Obtaining an accurate reading

Each group requires:
  ruler marked in cm

Q12 No.
Q13 That taken from position (*c*) because errors due to parallax are eliminated.
Q14 (*a*) 10, (*b*) 100.

The traditional metre standard definition is much preferred here to the SI definition, which involves the wavelengths in the spectrum of the krypton atom, because it is much more meaningful to pupils of this age.

Experiment 5.3   What is the thickness of a sheet of paper?

Each group requires:
  metre or half-metre rule
access to:
  a packet of 500 sheets of paper (for the purpose of this experiment
    one ream of paper (480 sheets) may be taken to contain 500
    sheets)
  some loose sheets of the same paper

Q15 0 mm.
Q16 500 times.

Pupils should realize that the thickness of one sheet of paper is too small to measure with accuracy. By taking a sufficiently large number of sheets, they should be able to measure accurately and so arrive, by calculation, at the thickness of one sheet.

Experiment 5.4   Mapping area

Material required:
  1 cm wooden cubes (16)

Q17 Area = length x breadth.

Q18 Carpets, land, glass, etc.
Q19 You have a temperature above normal.
Q20 No. Not as accurate as a thermometer.

Experiment 5.5   Putting the scale on (calibrating) a thermometer

Each group requires:
  beaker, 250 cm^3
  Bunsen burner
  distillation flask with stopper bored to take thermometer
  filter funnel
  gauze
  gummed labels (2)
  retort stand, clamp, and ring
  tripod
  unmarked thermometer (obtainable from usual laboratory suppliers)
  ice

At this stage, pupils will not have done enough work to understand
the principle of the hypsometer to determine the upper fixed point so
this is better left until later.

Q21 100 °C.

Experiment 5.6   Using a thermometer

Each group requires:
  thermometer from Experiment 5.5 or, if preferred, commercial one
    reading up to 110 °C

A warning should be given here about the limitations of the
thermometer — 'No attempting to take the temperature of the Bunsen
flame!'

Experiment 5.7   Using a lever-arm balance

Each group requires access to:
  lever-arm balance
  suitable objects for weighing

No attempt has been made to introduce the *newton* as a unit of force
here, nor to distinguish between mass and weight. These, in the
opinion of the authors, are better left until later and are dealt with
when forces are discussed in Book 2.

Experiment 5.8   A guessing game

Each group requires:
stopwatch
thermometer, 110 °C maximum
access to:
lever-arm balance

Other things to do

1 In this type of clock provision is made for altering the effective
length of the pendulum by adjusting the position of the bob (weight).
Raising the bob shortens the time of swing and so makes the clock go
faster; lowering the bob has the opposite effect.

2 The area of a football pitch is between 4200 m^2 and 11 000 m^2.
The area of a hockey pitch is approximately 5000 m^2.

3 Yorkshire.

4 The result to reject would be 1000 cm. The pupil has probably
confused centimetres with millimetres. If the measurement was
correct to the nearest millimetre, the result 100 cm would have been
more correctly expressed as 100.0 cm as this implies accuracy to
0.1 cm.

5 Take, for example, the map of Spain drawn in an atlas to a scale of
3 cm to 150 km. The approximate area of Spain on the map is 13 cm x
15 cm = 195 cm^2. As 1 cm represents 50 km, then 195 cm^2 represent
195 x 50 x 50 km^2. Spain is therefore approximately 487 500 km^2 in
area.

6 Volume and density

An exhibition of various containers to show volume/mass relationships is suggested to help introduce this topic.

Experiment 6.1   Finding the volumes of metal blocks

Each group requires:
    1 cm wooden cubes (50)
access to:
    blocks of various metals such as iron, lead, and aluminium in various sizes: e.g. 10 x 2 x 2 cm, 5 x 5 x 2 cm

   Q1   Volume = length x breadth x height, but only for these shapes.

Experiment 6.2   Does changing the shape alter the volume?

Each group requires:
    razor blade (single edge)
    ruler marked in cm
    plasticine (8 cm^3)

Great care must be taken in making the 1 cm cubes of plasticine as accurate as possible.

   Q2   Eight.
   Q3 8 cm^3.
   Q4 8 cm^3.
   Q5   No.

Experiment 6.3   Another way of measuring volume

Each group requires:
    measuring cylinder, 10 cm^3
    20 cm lengths of wooden dowel of diameter just to fit into 10 cm^3
        measuring cylinder (2)
    wooden rolling boards, 20 cm x 20 cm x 2.5 cm thick
    plasticine (8 cm^3)
    razor blade (single edge)
    talcum powder

The purpose of the experiment is to correlate the marking on the measuring cylinder with the 1 cm³ blocks of plasticine with which the pupils are familiar.

To make it easier to remove the plasticine from the cylinder, it has been found useful either to dust the plasticine cylinder with talc or to incorporate a thin wire 'wick' as shown in figure 6.1. Alternatively, the plasticine may be rolled to the correct diameter and held by the side of the scale on the cylinder.

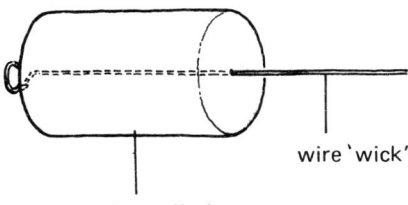

wire 'wick'

Figure 6.1   plasticine cylinder

Q6 8 cm³.
Q7 8 (cm³).
Q8 cm³.
Q9 5 cm³.

Experiment 6.4   Measuring volume using a displacement can

Each group requires:
    displacement can
    gauze
    measuring cylinder, 50 cm³
    tripod
    object labelled 'X' — this must be one of the metal blocks used in
        Experiment 6.1 so that the volume is already known

Q10 Yes.

The experiment may profitably be extended using other objects of irregular shape.

Experiment 6.5   Finding the mass of blocks of equal volume

Each group requires:
    blocks of Perspex, wood, and aluminium, 10 x 2 x 2 cm
access to:
    Butchart balance

Q11 2 g/cm³.
Q12 0.5 g/cm³.

Experiment 6.6   Finding densities

Each group requires:
    displacement can
    gauze
    measuring cylinder, 50 cm^3
    metre rule
    tripod
    blocks of various materials and sizes (see below)
access to:
    Butchart balance

Similar blocks to those used in Experiment 6.1 are appropriate but other materials and sizes should be included if possible. Ideally, blocks of the same material but different volume should be included.

Q13 By finding the mass of a container when 'empty' and then again with the liquid in it.
Q14 Using a measuring cylinder.

Demonstration experiment 6A   To show that air has mass

Use the apparatus shown in figure 6.2.

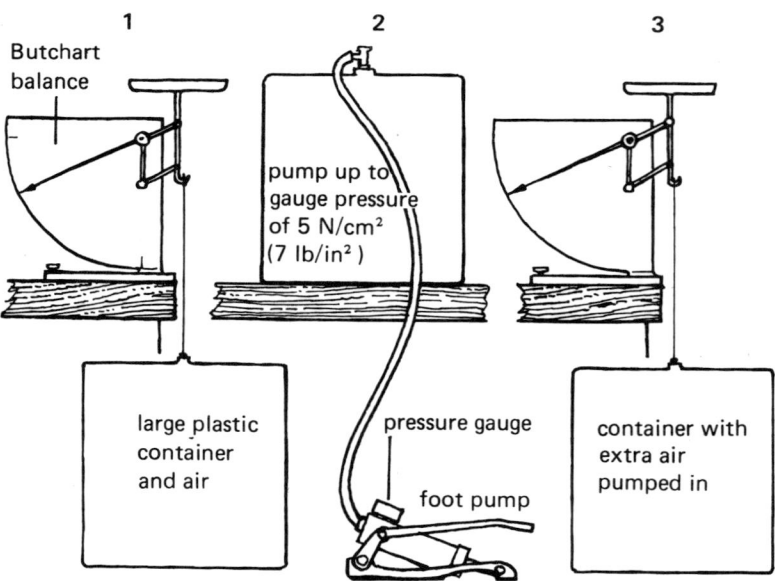

Figure 6.2

Alternative method

If the suggested apparatus is not available the following more
traditional method could be used.

1 Find the mass of a 1000 cm³ round-
bottomed flask fitted up as shown
in figure 6.3.
2 Evacuate the flask.
3 Find its mass again.
4 Open the tap under water.
5 When no more water enters, close
the tap.
6 Pour the water into a 1000 cm³
measuring cylinder to determine
the volume of air pumped out.

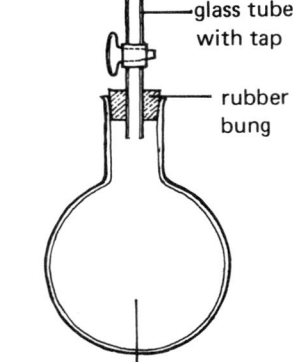

Figure 6.3   round-bottomed flask

Ideally a balance reading accurate to three places of decimals is
needed for this experiment to give a reasonable result.

Q15 Yes.

Demonstration experiment 6B   To find the density of air

The alternative method for the experiment above could of course be
used here also. However, experience has shown that the following
method is better and has more impact.

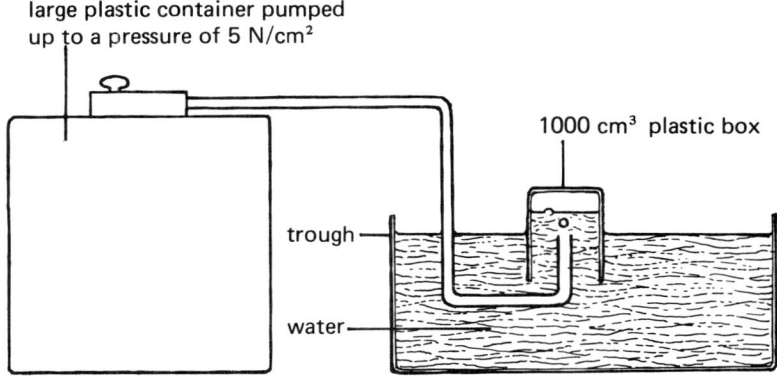

Figure 6.4

Set up the apparatus shown in figure 6.4.

1 Find the mass of the container of air pumped up to a pressure of
5 N/cm² (7 lb/in² approximately) as in the previous demonstration.
2 Remove ten 1000 cm³ boxes full of air by the method indicated in
the diagram.
3 Find the mass of the container again.

Using a pressure of 5 N/cm² ensures that 10 litres of air can be removed
so eliminating difficult arithmetic.

Other things to do

1 B 5 g/cm³; C 5 cm³; D 54 g; E 0.8 g/cm³.

2 B will go down. If water stays on top of the liquid 'L' in B, then L
must be denser than water. Bottle B will then be heavier than bottle A
as they contain equal volumes of liquid.

3 The petrol tanker is larger because petrol is less dense than cement
and therefore occupies a greater volume for the same mass.

4 By determining the volume and mass of the crown and hence its
density. The density should then be compared with those of pure gold
and pure silver. If there were any silver in the crown, the density
would be less than 19.3 g per cm³.

5 The difficulty here is finding the volume of the cork because cork
floats in water. This is overcome by attaching an iron 'sinker' to the
cork and then finding the volume of sinker plus cork using a
displacement can. The volume of the sinker alone may be found in the
same way, and hence that of the cork.

7 Heating things

Experiment 7.1   Melting and boiling

Each group requires:
beaker, 100 cm^3
Bunsen burner
gauze
tripod
ice cube

The object here is first to melt the ice and then to boil the water
formed so as to observe two distinct changes of state. Unless pupils
are instructed to heat slowly and carefully and to observe everything,
one of these changes may be missed.

Q1 It melted to a liquid (water).
Q2 It changed to a gas (steam) – it boiled.
Q3 'When ice is heated it *melts* and changes into *water* which is a
liquid. When the *water* is heated further it *boils* and *steam* is formed.'
Q4 Sublimation. Example: naphthalene (or ammonium chloride or
iodine). (This is a reference back to Experiment 3.6.)

Demonstration experiment 7A   To show the change in volume when water changes to steam

Materials required:
beakers (tall-form), 1000 cm^3 (2)
Bunsen burners (2)
gauzes (2)
glass syringe, 100 cm^3
hypodermic syringe, 1 cm^3 (1 ml) calibrated in 0.1 cm^3 (0.1 ml)
    divisions
retort stand and clamp
rubber cap ('policeman') to fit over end of glass syringe
tripods (2)
saturated sodium chloride solution (brine)

1 Set up the apparatus as shown in figure 7.1.
2 Have the water and the brine boiling before the beginning of the
lesson.

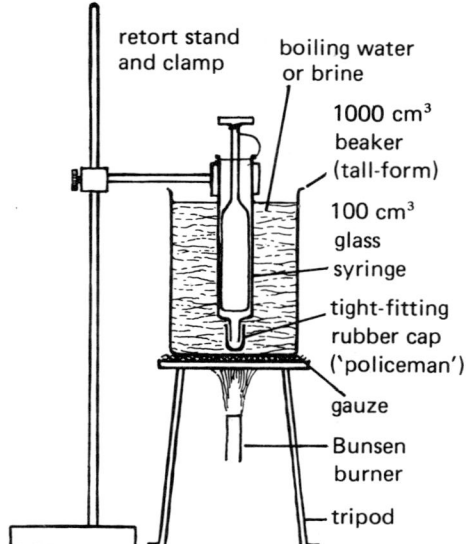

Figure 7.1

3 Push the piston of the syringe to the bottom and fit the rubber cap.
4 Immerse as much of the syringe as possible in the beaker of boiling water for at least five minutes. (This also could have been done before the lesson.)
5 When the syringe has reached the temperature of the water, remove it from the beaker, pierce the rubber cap with the hypodermic needle, and introduce 0.1 cm³ (0.1 ml) of water into the syringe.
6 Immerse the syringe as completely as possible in the boiling brine and observe what happens. (If necessary, gently twist the piston to free it should it be found to stick.)
7 Record the volume of steam formed. It should approach 100 cm³ (100 ml), i.e. a 1000 times increase from the 0.1 cm³ of water introduced.
8 Remove the syringe from the brine and allow it to cool to show the great decrease in volume when the steam condenses.
9 The heating and cooling may be repeated if desired.

Q5 About 1000 times.

Although, up to this point, the particulate nature of matter has not been touched upon, it could profitably be introduced in a very elementary form here without supporting evidence. (Most pupils are already aware of the existence of atoms.) A three-dimensional kinetic theory model, such as the one shown in figure 7.2, is a useful way of demonstrating the differences between a liquid and a gas in terms of the particulate theory. (A solid cannot be satisfactorily simulated in this way.)

Figure 7.2
A three-dimensional
kinetic theory model.

Experiment 7.2   A little becomes a lot

Each group requires:
    rubber band or string
    small transparent plastic bag or small balloon
    solid carbon dioxide – obtained from a carbon dioxide cylinder
        with dry ice attachment

SAFETY. Do not touch the solid carbon dioxide or allow pupils to do
so: it can cause serious 'burns'. Handle the pieces with forceps.

Q6 The bag swells.
Q7 It has changed into a gas and there has been a considerable
increase in volume. If kinetic theory has been introduced, an
explanation in terms of the particles may be given by some pupils.

Experiment 7.3   Heating various substances

Each group requires:
    asbestos mat
    Bunsen burner
    hard-glass test-tubes, 100 x 16 mm
    test-tube holder (wooden clothes pegs are satisfactory and cheap)
    tongs
    suitable substances for heating such as:
        aluminium foil (10 cm squares)   red lead
        cobalt chloride crystals   salt (sodium chloride)
        copper foil (2 cm squares)   solder
        copper(II) sulphate crystals
        crushed coal
        lead foil (1 cm squares)
        magnesium ribbon (5 cm lengths)
        potassium permanganate

The actual results are less important than the experience of heating and test of observation at this stage.

The method of heating shown in figure 7.3b in the students' book has the advantage that molten metals, etc. fall on to the asbestos mat and not either on to the bench or down the chimney of the Bunsen.

SAFETY. The magnesium flame is very bright and pupils should be warned not to look directly at it.

The substances suggested would group as follows:

a *Substances which change state on heating but return to their original state when cool, that is, no new substance is formed:*

lead foil (by this method of heating it is unlikely that any yellow
  lead(II) oxide will be formed; if some is formed then lead would be
  placed in group b)
solder

b *New substance formed:*

aluminium foil — white oxide coating
cobalt chloride crystals — change from pink to blue
copper foil — black coating of oxide (green tinged Bunsen flame
  during the heating)
*copper(II) sulphate crystals — change from blue crystals to white
  powder (anhydrous copper(II) sulphate)
magnesium ribbon — brilliant white flame; white powder formed
  (magnesium oxide)
potassium permanganate — black powder (manganese(IV) oxide)
  formed; decrepitates; oxygen evolved
red lead — yellow powder (lead(II) oxide) formed; oxygen evolved

c *No change:*

crushed coal (unless temperature reached is high enough to drive off
  volatile products)
sodium chloride (salt)

*It is felt that at this stage merely 'copper sulphate' is sufficient for the pupils; copper(II) sulphate should not be insisted upon.

Experiment 7.4   Heating copper sulphate crystals

Each group requires:
  beaker, 250 cm^3
  Bunsen burner
  delivery tube as in figure 7.3, fitted with no. 13 rubber stopper
  hard-glass test-tube (A), 100 x 16 mm
  retort stand and clamp

soda-glass test-tube (B)
fine crystals of copper(II) sulphate-5-water
  (crushed cobalt chloride crystals if experiment is repeated)

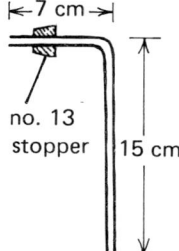

Figure 7.3

Additional materials for tests in table 7.2.
  asbestos paper
  thermometer, −10 to 110 °C
  tongs
  distilled water
  ethanol (industrial methylated spirits)
  sodium chloride solution (say 5%)

Notes in the students' book

a The reason for this is to prevent the water given off, which
condenses on the cooler parts of the tube, running back on to the hot
glass and cracking it.
d Special attention should be given to this as many pupils are careless
about it and the result is often burned fingers.

Q8 Blue before; white powder after.
Q9 Pupils may conclude that the liquid is water which would be
wrong as, at this stage, there is no evidence to support this
conclusion. The only valid conclusion is that a colourless liquid has
collected.
Q10 Water. Pupils are expected to suggest determination of boiling
point as they have met this as a criterion of purity in Chapter 3.
For this reason, thermometers are included in the list of additional
materials above.

It may be worth while, at this point, to deal with the use of anhydrous
copper(II) sulphate (or cobalt chloride paper) as a test for the presence
of water and to make it clear that neither of these substances
provides a specific test for water. The only ways of showing that a
particular liquid is water are by the determination of its boiling point
(100 °C at a pressure of one atmosphere) and freezing point or
density.

Q11 Pupils should notice the considerable amount of heat evolved when water is added to anhydrous copper(II) sulphate. It can be explained in terms of the energy given out when the two combine together chemically (hydration energy of the copper(II) ion).

Q12 Similarities: water is evolved; heat is given out when water is added to the anhydrous salt. Differences: colour change (pink to blue).

Experiment 7.5 Is there a change in mass when magnesium is heated?

Each group requires:
  Bunsen burner
  crucible and lid
  pipeclay triangle
  tongs
  tripod
  emery paper
  magnesium ribbon, 30 cm
access to:
  balance capable of weighing to at least two decimal places
    (preferably a top-pan variety for speed of operation)

Alternative method. As an alternative, copper foil or wire may be used in this experiment. If this is done, copper should be substituted for magnesium in Experiment 8.1 and Demonstration Experiments 8A and 8B to preserve the consistency of the argument.

Q13 Yes.

Q14 It increases.

Q15 Using a 30 cm length of magnesium ribbon, an increase of the order of 0.2 g can be expected.

Q16 Some pupils, through carelessness or faulty technique, will get a loss in mass but the class average as a whole ought to show an increase. Disparities can be used to underline the importance of repeating experiments several times before coming to any definite conclusions.

Q17 To admit more air (oxygen).

Experiment 7.6 Is there a change in mass when red lead is heated?

Each group requires:
  Bunsen burner
  crucible (without lid) as an alternative to test-tube
  hard-glass test-tube, 100 x 16 mm

retort stand and clamp
spatula
tripod and pipeclay triangle as alternatives to retort stand
red lead
access to:
balance as used in Experiment 7.5

The same apparatus may be used as in Experiment 7.5 (although crucible lids are not necessary) or the apparatus shown in figure 7.4.

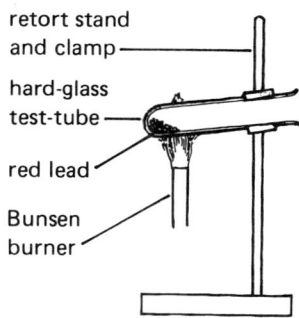

retort stand
and clamp

hard-glass
test-tube

red lead

Bunsen
burner

Figure 7.4

Q18 Yes.
Q19 It decreases.
Q20 With about 10 g of red lead, a decrease of the order of 0.2 g may be expected.
Q21 Similar considerations apply as to question 16 above and similar errors may arise.
Q22 Magnesium is gaining something and red lead is losing something.

Other things to do

1 The outside of the jar becomes misty because of condensation. This is due to the cold air near the jar not being able to hold as much moisture as the warm air.

3 With the air hole closed the gas is burning in air. With the air hole open a gas/air mixture is being burnt in air, which burns more fiercely.

8 What is air?

Experiment 8.1   Does red lead give off a gas when heated?

Each group requires:
  asbestos mat
  Bunsen burner
  hard-glass test-tube, 100 x 16 mm
  spatula
  test-tube holder
  wooden splint
  red lead

  Q1 Yes.
  Q2 No, because a glowing splint does not relight in air.

Experiment 8.2   Investigating the gas given off when red lead is heated

Each group requires:
  Bunsen burner
  corks to fit test-tubes (2)
  glass delivery tube as in figure 8.1, fitted with no. 13 rubber
      stopper
  hard-glass test-tubes, 100 x 16 mm (3)
  pneumatic trough or plastic bowl
  retort stand and clamp
  tongs
  wooden splint
  magnesium ribbon, 5 cm
  red lead

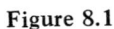

no. 13 rubber stopper

Figure 8.1

The notes in the pupils' book need careful attention.

  Q3 It relit.
  Q4 Brighter in the gas than in air.
  Q5 A white solid. This solid was formed in experiments in which magnesium was burned in air.

Experiment 8.3   Burning magnesium in air

Each group requires:
Bunsen burner
tongs
magnesium ribbon (sufficient to ensure that some remains
    unburnt, e.g. 5 cm)

Experiment 8.4   How much air is used when magnesium burns?

Each group requires:
beaker, 250 cm³
hard-glass tube, 15 x 2.5 cm approx. (a boiling-tube with the bottom
    cut off will serve well here)
10 cm length of glass rod to fit stopper
retort stand and clamp
rubber stopper, no. 23, with one hole
wooden splint
adhesive tape
magnesium ribbon, 5 cm

Q6 It continued to burn but then went out.
Q7 It went up.
Q8 No. (*a*) $\frac{1}{5}$.
Q9 The splint stopped burning. The air that was left would not
allow things to burn in it.
Q10 So that all the 'active' part of the air (oxygen) is used up.

A more accurate method of determining the percentage of oxygen in
the air is given below.

Demonstration experiment 8A   Determining the percentage of oxygen in the air

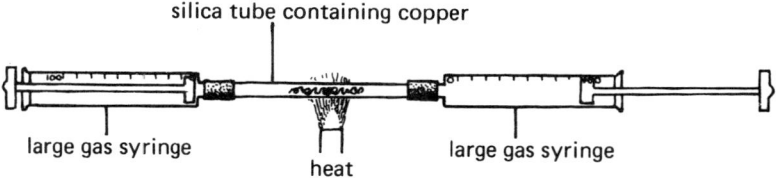

silica tube containing copper

large gas syringe

heat

large gas syringe

Figure 8.2

The apparatus is shown in figure 8.2. The silica tube contains freshly
reduced wire-form copper(II) oxide. This is prepared as described below.
One of the syringes contains 100 cm³ of air and the other has the

piston set at 0 cm³. The copper is heated strongly and the air continually passed through it from one syringe to the other. After several passes the gas should be allowed to remain in the first syringe and its volume measured. The volume of gas remaining should be approximately 80 cm³. The copper in the silica tube goes black due to formation of copper(II) oxide.

Reduction of copper(II) oxide wire

The apparatus shown in figure 8.3 is needed. Care should be taken that all the air is swept out of the tube before the hydrogen is ignited. The tube should be heated strongly and the excess hydrogen burned at the end of the tube. When the black copper(II) oxide has been reduced to copper (red), then the heating can stop but the hydrogen must still be passed through the tube whilst cooling is taking place in order to prevent re-oxidation.

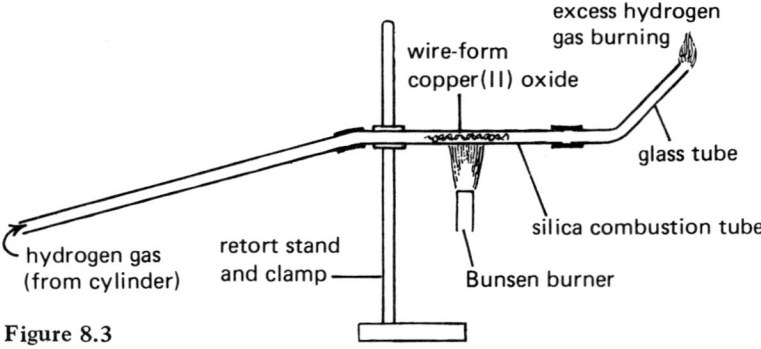

Figure 8.3

Explaining burning

It is not intended here to give a rigid definition of the term 'compound' or to distinguish it from 'element'. This distinction will be drawn in Book 2.

Experiment 8.5 Investigating oxides

Each group requires:
  combustion spoon
  corks to fit test-tubes (2)
  delivery tube
  pneumatic trough or plastic bowl
  spatula
  test-tubes, 100 x 25 mm (2)
  distilled water

calcium metal turnings
magnesium ribbon
powdered charcoal
powdered roll sulphur
steel wool
universal indicator solution or papers
access to:
oxygen cylinder or generator

Q11 'Oxides of metals are either *alkaline* or *neutral* in solution in water, whereas oxides of non-metals are *acidic* in solution in water.'

Experiment 8.6 Detecting carbon dioxide

Each group requires:
delivery tubes as in figure 8.4
rubber stoppers, no. 23, with two holes (3)
test-tubes, 150 x 25 mm (3)
limewater
access to:
filter pump attached to water tap
source of carbon dioxide

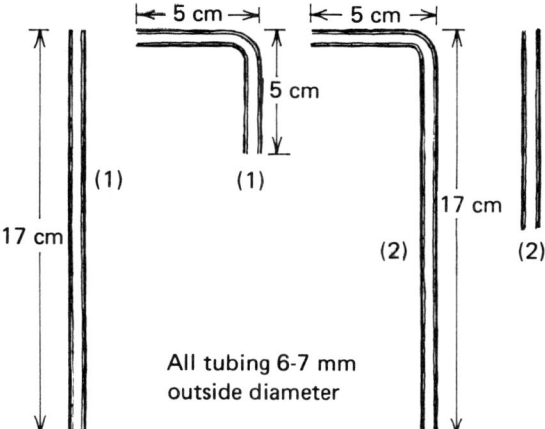

Figure 8.4

The experiment should be preceded by a demonstration of the limewater test for carbon dioxide.

The control experiment using tube B could be carried out as a demonstration. The room air can be safely bubbled through limewater for five minutes without the atmospheric carbon dioxide affecting it.

Q12 (*a*) It goes milky. (*b*) There is little change.

Q13 Less. Pupils are likely to think, *on the evidence of this experiment,* that there is no carbon dioxide in the air of the room. This introduces the possibility of its not being detected and therefore the need for a more sensitive indicator.

Experiment 8.7   Another way of detecting carbon dioxide

Each group requires:
    delivery tubes as in figure 8.5
    rubber stoppers, no. 23, with two holes (2)
    test-tubes, 150 x 25 mm (2)
    'bicarbonate indicator'
access to:
    filter pump attached to water tap
    source of carbon dioxide

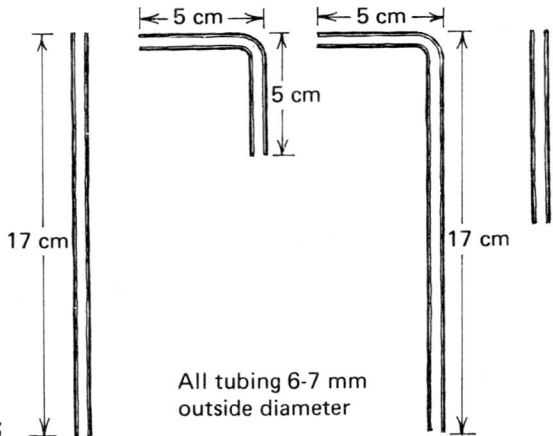

Figure 8.5

Making up 'bicarbonate indicator'

Stock solution:
1 Dissolve 0.2 g thymol blue and 0.1 g cresol red in 20 cm^3 industrial methylated spirits.
2 Weigh out 0.84 g sodium hydrogen carbonate (A.R. quality) and dissolve this in about 900 cm^3 of distilled water.
3 Add the dye solution to the aqueous solution in a one litre graduated flask and make up to the one litre mark with distilled water. Take care to exclude all traces of dust and dirt, as these can have a marked effect on the final colours the indicator will produce.

Working solution: Pipette 25 cm^3 of the stock solution into a 250 cm^3 graduated flask, and make up the volume to 250 cm^3 with distilled water.

Experiment 8.8 Do other animals breathe out carbon dioxide?

Each group requires:
metal gauze cage
rubber stopper, no. 23
test-tube, 150 x 25 mm
'bicarbonate indicator'
locust 'hoppers' (or worms could be used) (1 or 2)

Q14 Yes. The 'bicarbonate indicator' changes colour.

Control experiment. Exactly the same but without the animals being present.

Experiment 8.9 Do plants breathe out carbon dioxide?

Each group requires:
gauze to hold pieces of potato
rubber stoppers, no. 23 (4)
test-tubes, 150 x 25 mm (4)
aluminium foil
'bicarbonate indicator'
green leaves (2)
pieces of potato

Material used	Colour of indicator	
	start	finish
potato in the dark	purple–pink	yellow
potato in the light	purple–pink	yellow
green leaf in the dark	purple–pink	yellow
green leaf in the light	purple–pink	purple–pink

Table 8.1

Q15 (*a*) Yes. (*b*) Yes, in the dark, but not in the light.
Q16 Carbon dioxide is being given out by the plants in the dark and oxygen is being used up. In practice, the amounts involved are not likely to have any adverse effects on the patients.

Experiment 8.10   Is all or only part of the oxygen used up in breathing?

Each group requires:
    gas burette
    hypodermic syringe to hold 1 cm^3
    lengths of rubber tubing (2)
    pneumatic trough or plastic bowl
    Suba-seal cap for gas burette
    U-tube with stoppers
    alkaline pyrogallol solution (see below)
    granulated soda lime

Pupils may need to be told, in part 3 of this experiment, that water is let into the burette by opening the tap slightly and closing it again when the required amount has entered.

Injection of the pyrogallol should be done by the teacher because of the strongly alkaline solution. The method is indicated in figure 8.6.

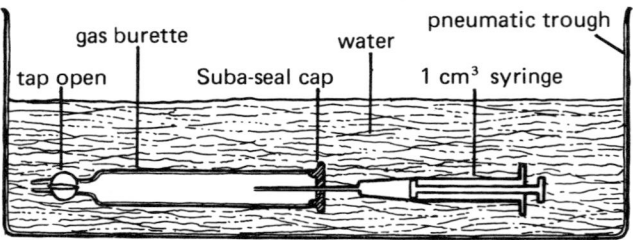

Figure 8.6 Injection of pyrogallol.

Making up alkaline pyrogallol

Mix together one volume of dry potassium hydroxide pellets and five volumes of dry pyrogallol powder. Now pour over the mixture simultaneously two volumes of water and one volume of liquid paraffin.

If this is carried out carefully, an almost colourless solution results with the paraffin uppermost forming a seal against atmospheric oxygen. A brown coloration indicates that oxygen has been absorbed.

Demonstration experiment 8B   To show that exhaled air contains oxygen

This experiment may be used to demonstrate that exhaled air contains oxygen. Many pupils think that all the oxygen is used up and therefore exhaled breath does not contain oxygen.

To convince the pupils that the fall of the piston is not due to gravity a control syringe should be set up alongside. If this contains

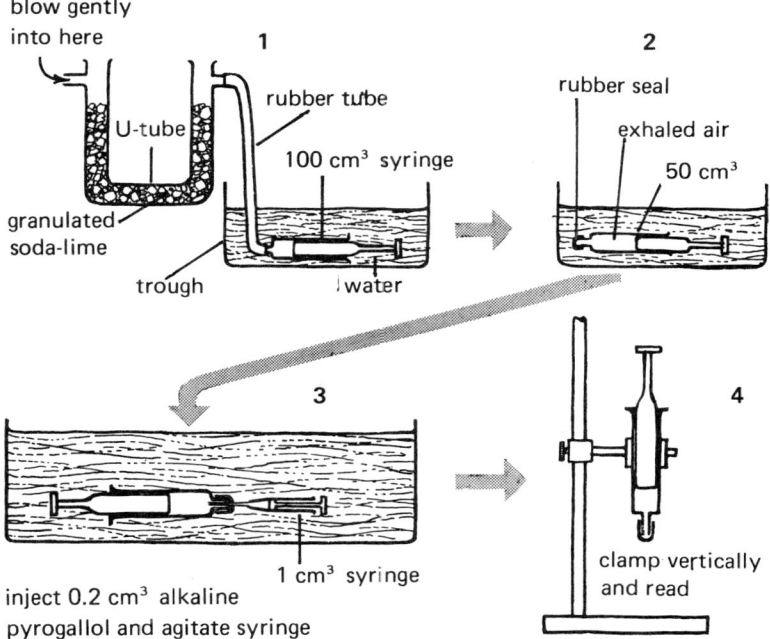

Figure 8.7

the same amount of air as taken in the first case it will not show any decrease, that is, the piston will not fall appreciably.

Q17 Only part.

Q18 Exhaled air.

Q19 A reasonable amount of oxygen (a minimum of 12 per cent oxygen is necessary for mouth to mouth resuscitation to be effective). Experiment 8.10 shows that exhaled air does contain a fairly high proportion of oxygen.

Experiment 8.11   Discovering air pressure

Each group requires:
    beaker, 250 cm³, without lip
    glass or plastic tube, 1 m long, 12 mm bore
    rubber tubing to fit above tube
    screw clip
    stiff card to fit over top of beaker

Q20 The water level drops.

Q21 The pressure of the air is supporting it.

Q22 It is held in by the card which is supported by air pressure.

Demonstration experiment 8C   The water fountain effect

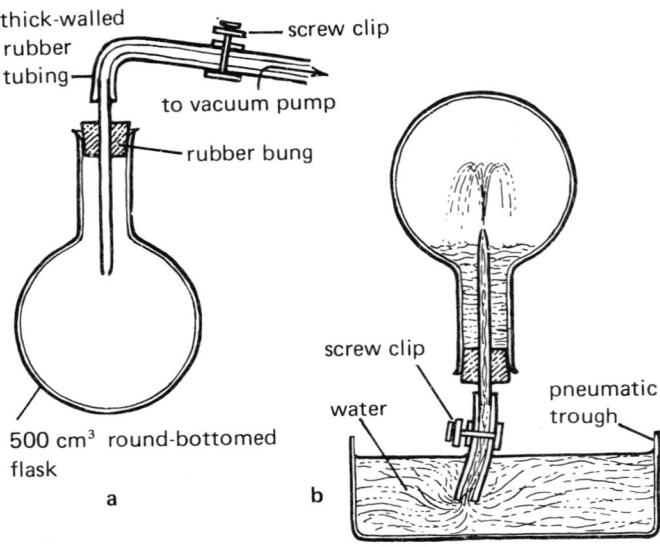

thick-walled
rubber
tubing

screw clip

to vacuum pump

rubber bung

500 cm³ round-bottomed
flask

a

screw clip

water

b

pneumatic
trough

Figure 8.8

Set up the apparatus as in figure 8.8a. Evacuate the flask for about
two minutes. Then arrange the apparatus as in figure 8.8b and open
the clip.
It is worth while to show the effect of inverting the flask in water,
with the clip open, before evacuating it when, of course, the water does
not rise. On repeating with the flask evacuated a fountain effect is
achieved.

Demonstration experiment 8D   A dramatic demonstration of air pressure

Evacuate the metal can as shown in figure 8.9.
This demonstrates the force of the atmospheric air which causes the
metal to collapse. The experiment can be carried out using washing-up-
liquid containers which will regain their shape when air is allowed to
re-enter.

Q23 Air pressure on the surface of the water in the beaker pushes
the water up.
Q24 The air pressure is greater on the outside than on the inside
of the can.

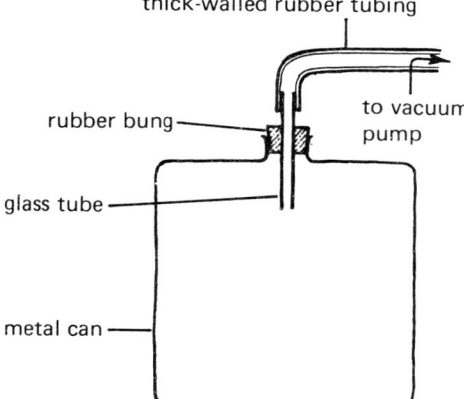

Figure 8.9

Demonstration experiment 8E   Making a simple barometer

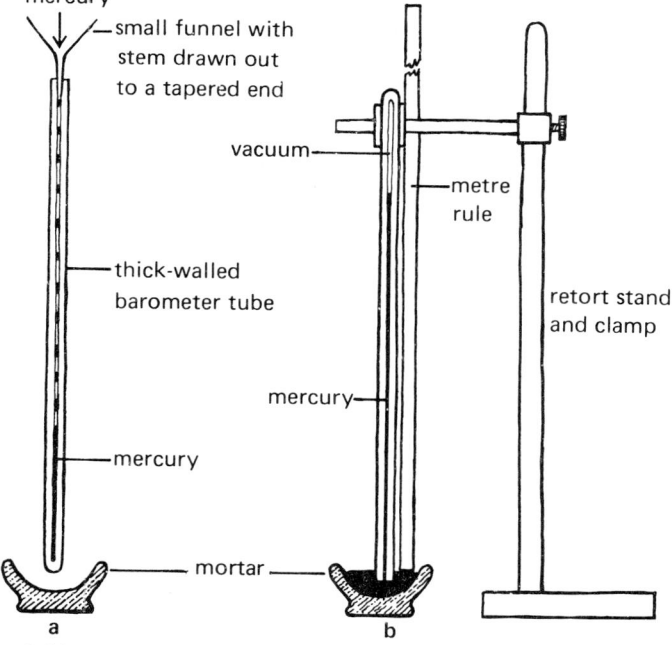

Figure 8.10

1   Fill the tube to approximately 1 cm from the top with clean mercury (figure 8.10a). Close the open end with the thumb and carefully invert the tube several times to remove trapped air.
2   Use a teat pipette to fill the remaining part of the tube with mercury.

3 Hold the thumb firmly over the open end of the tube and invert it into a mortar of mercury. Remove the thumb and clamp the tube vertically (figure 8.10b).

Q25 The length of the barometer tube would have to be 13.6 times longer.

Demonstration experiment 8F   Making a 'water barometer'

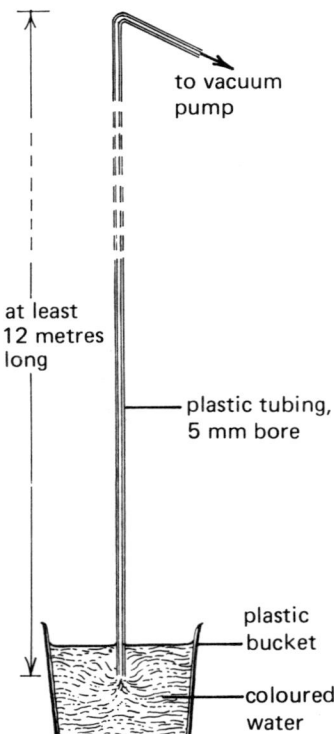

Figure 8.11

Figure 8.11 shows the apparatus set up for making a 'water barometer'. This may conveniently be set up in the well of a staircase or through a laboratory window.

Note. A cheap card is obtainable from Negretti & Zamba Ltd., which is an aid to local weather forecasting.

Q26 On the face of the barometer, high pressure indicates fair weather and so on.

Experiment 8.12   Plotting air pressure

Each group requires:
graph paper
access to:
aneroid barometer

Q27 It should agree broadly.
Q28 a The greater atmospheric pressure forces the ink into the sac.
b The greater atmospheric air pressure forces a flow of air containing dust into the cleaner.
c The greater atmospheric air pressure forces air into the lungs.
Q29 *Figure 8.28* Compressed air forces the drill into the ground.
Figure 8.29 As there is no pressure in space compressed air carried by the astronaut is forced into the lungs.
Figure 8.30 Because air can be compressed a large quantity can be carried in a small container.
Figure 8.31 Compressed air provides a springy cushion on which the craft rides.

Other things to do

1 *Some uses of compressed air:* driving some types of motors where sparks may cause explosions, underwater work such as skin diving, bicycle pumps, air sprays, sandblasting, temporary inflatable buildings.

2 *Some uses of reduced pressure:* kitchen extractor fans, drinking straws, car radiator fans, medical syringes, aneroid barometers, commercial jam making (reducing the air pressure makes the jam boil at a lower temperature, thus preserving flavour).

9 Water

Samples of many 'different kinds' of water will be required for the first experiment of this chapter. As wide a range of samples as possible should be collected (river water, pond water, etc.). No attempt should be made to remove material such as weeds and mud found in the water. The samples should be clearly labelled with their origin.

Distilled water and temporary hard water must be included among the samples and will have to be supplied by the teacher. The temporary hard water may conveniently be prepared by bubbling carbon dioxide into limewater until the white precipitate which forms just redissolves. Filter if necessary.

Pupils should be encouraged to bring in their own water samples.

Experiment 9.1   A closer look at water

Each group requires:
    microscope slide
    suitable containers, e.g. 100 cm^3 beakers
    samples of 'different kinds' of water as explained above
    other apparatus as required by the pupils

Q3 Methods of purifying the water such as filtering will not, of course, remove the dissolved solids. Therefore, almost certainly the samples are still not the same although they may look similar.

Evaporating. If an infra-red lamp is available, this is preferable to heating the microscope slide with a Bunsen burner. If a Bunsen is used a warning should be given to the pupils about the size of the flame so as to avoid cracking the slide.

Q4 Solid material dissolved from the land over which the water has flowed, or from the air.
Q5 Principally in the South Downs and Derbyshire, but there are several others.
Q6 White solid.

Experiment 9.2   Getting soap to lather

Each group requires:
    Bunsen burner
    teat pipette

test-tubes, 100 x 16 mm (2)
test-tube holder
test-tube rack
pure soap solution (e.g. solution of Lux soap flakes) — detergents, such as washing-up liquid and certain washing powders, must **NOT** be used
solution A — distilled water
solution B — temporary hard water (see Experiment 9.1)

Q7 A, distilled water.
Q8 Because the water in B has something dissolved in it. (It is likely to be chalk or limestone but pupils will of course not know this.)
Q9 There should now be little difference between A and B. The reason is that calcium hydrogen carbonate, the cause of the hardness in B, has been converted, by the heating, into calcium carbonate which is insoluble and cannot, therefore, cause hardness.
Q10 As far as the pupils are concerned, boiling has removed the impurity which prevented the formation of a lather.

Hardness of water

This section is included for the teacher's benefit; it may be too difficult for the pupils at this stage.

The scum that is formed with hard water and soap is due to the formation of an insoluble calcium salt of the soap. If the soap is sodium stearate (one of the common soaps) the scum is of calcium stearate:

soap	+	calcium ions	$\longrightarrow$	calcium stearate
(sodium stearate)		(present in hard water)		(scum)
soluble		soluble		insoluble

No lather can be formed until all the calcium ions have been removed in this way from the water. This requires a great deal of soap.

The hard water may be 'temporarily hard', that is the hardness is temporary and can be removed by boiling alone. This type of hardness is commonly due to the presence of dissolved calcium hydrogen carbonate (bicarbonate). It is formed by rain water containing dissolved carbon dioxide reacting with the limestone (calcium carbonate) of the rocks over which it has run. The reaction is:

$CaCO_3$	+	H_2O	+	CO_2	$\longrightarrow$	$Ca(HCO_3)_2$
calcium carbonate		water		carbon dioxide		calcium hydrogen
(limestone)				(dissolved in the water)		carbonate
insoluble						soluble

If this temporary hard water is boiled the above reaction is reversed so insoluble calcium carbonate is formed and all the calcium ions are removed from the solution. Lathering can then take place with soap.

The hard water may, alternatively, be 'permanently hard' in which case the dissolved impurity responsible for the hardness is commonly calcium sulphate. Although almost insoluble (about 1 part in 500 parts of water), calcium sulphate will dissolve sufficiently for the calcium ions which it contains to cause hardness. This substance cannot be removed simply by boiling — hence the name 'permanent hard water'. The calcium sulphate is dissolved into the water from rocks containing the mineral gypsum ($CaSO_4.2H_2O$). To soften permanent hard water sodium carbonate may be added. This reacts with the dissolved calcium sulphate as follows:

$$CaSO_4 \quad + \quad Na_2CO_3 \quad \rightarrow \quad CaCO_3 \quad + \quad Na_2SO_4$$

calcium sulphate sodium carbonate calcium carbonate sodium sulphate
slightly soluble   soluble   insoluble   soluble

Other methods are available for softening hard water of both types. The corresponding magnesium salts also cause hardness of water and have similar effects.

Soapless detergents form a lather with water irrespective of whether it is hard or not as there is no reaction between the dissolved calcium or magnesium compounds and the detergent.

Experiment 9.3   Adding things to water

Each group requires:
  spatula
  test-tubes, 100 x 16 mm
  test-tube rack
  suggested substances in labelled containers:
     calcium metal, common salt, disinfectant, flour, lithium metal, sand, sugar, etc.

Pupils should be advised to use small amounts of the substances only. The substances suggested fall into three types: (*a*) those which are soluble in water, (*b*) those which are insoluble in water, and (*c*) those which react with water.

Q11 All traces of solid should have disappeared.
Q12 By filtering or evaporating the solution in those cases where no reaction occurs, the solid should be regained.

Experiment 9.4   A closer look at calcium and water

Each group requires:
    beaker, 250 cm^3
    cork to fit test-tube
    test-tube, 100 x 16 mm
    wooden splint
    anhydrous copper sulphate
    calcium metal turnings
    distilled water
    universal indicator paper

Q13   No.
Q14   On lighting the gas, a mild explosion ('pop') should occur. (This is a distinctive test for hydrogen.)
Q15   From the water. Calcium, of course, is an element. Pupils may find the effervescence (fizzing) of the calcium misleading.
Q16   They would expect the pH to be 7.
Q17   It is alkaline. In fact it will have a pH of 10+ because of the formation of alkaline calcium hydroxide.
Q18   Calcium + water gives *hydrogen* and an *alkaline solution.*

Demonstration experiment 9A   Burning hydrogen in air

Set up the apparatus shown in figure 9.1.

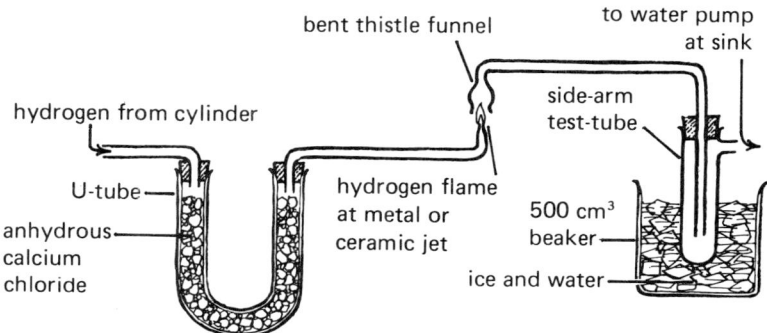

Figure 9.1

1   Turn on the hydrogen so that a steady, fairly slow stream of gas passes through the apparatus.
2   When all the air has been driven out of the apparatus, light the hydrogen at the jet and adjust the rate of flow of the gas so that the flame is about 3 cm high.
3   Turn on the water so that the products of combustion will be drawn into the side-arm test-tube.

4 After about ten minutes' heating, 2 to 3 cm depth of liquid will have collected in the test-tube.

> **Q19** A colourless liquid. (It is, of course, wrong to assume that it is water as there is no definite proof of this.)
> **Q20** Water, or a solution containing water.
> **Q21** Finding the freezing point, boiling point, or density.

Experiment 9.5   A look at magnesium and water

Each group requires (probably):
  beaker, 250 cm³
  Bunsen burner
  cork to fit test-tube
  test-tube, 100 x 16 mm
  wooden splint
  magnesium ribbon

> **Q22** Pupils will probably repeat the calcium experiment (9.4) without obtaining any hydrogen. (Hydrogen is formed by the reaction between cold water and magnesium but the rate of formation of hydrogen is so slow that pupils are unlikely to notice any bubbles – it is usually necessary to leave the apparatus for about one week to collect 5 cm³ or so of hydrogen.)

Experiment 9.6   Burning magnesium in steam

Each group requires:
  beaker, 250 cm³
  Bunsen burner
  delivery tube as in figure 9.2
  hard-glass test-tube, 150 x 25 mm
  retort stand and clamp
  rubber stopper, no. 23, with one hole
  test-tubes, 100 x 16 mm (2)
  Rocksill
  distilled water
  magnesium ribbon

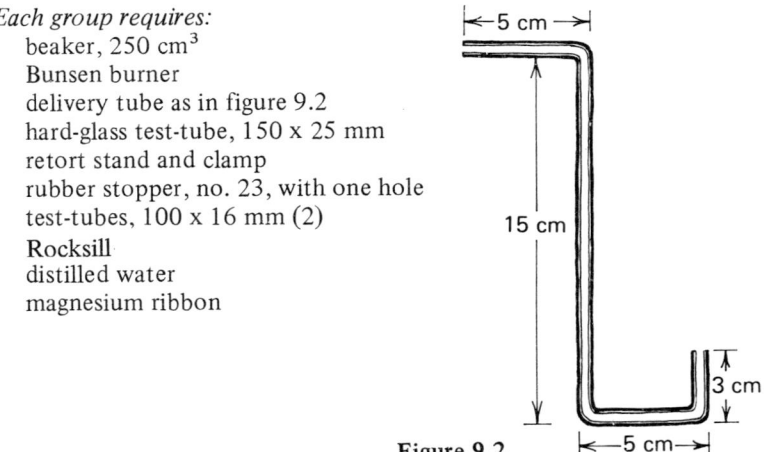

Figure 9.2

Stress the importance of not stopping the heating while the end of the delivery tube is under the water.

Q23 Hydrogen.
Q24 Magnesium oxide — oxides of metals are basic (alkaline).
Q25 Magnesium combined with oxygen which it took from the steam.
Q26 Hydrogen oxide.

Experiment 9.7   How important is water to plants?

Each group requires:
  crystallizing dishes or similar containers
    (saucers may be suitable) (6)
  measuring cylinder, 10 cm^3
  measuring cylinder, 50 cm^3
  John Innes potting compost No. 2
  oat seeds (alternatives — barley, wheat)

It will take the seedlings from seven to fourteen days to grow to a
height of 3 cm, depending on conditions.

Q27 Results will vary to some extent due to differences in the seed.
The most likely answers are dish 4 or 5.
Q28 20 cm^3 or 30 cm^3 (probably).
Q29 Dish 1.
Q30 None.
Q31 See results.

The pupils' bar chart should have the outline shape shown in figure 9.3.

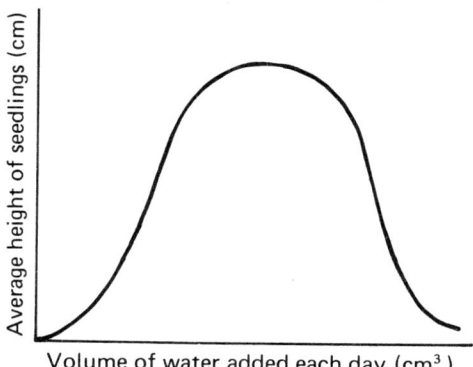

Figure 9.3   Volume of water added each day (cm^3)

As an alternative, especially for less able pupils, use could be made
again here of the statistics frame to avoid the arithmetic involved in
averaging. A graph could then be plotted from the outline shown on
the statistics frame.

Q32 Yes. Most likely this will be shown by the height of the
seedlings in dish 6.

Q33 Into the plant. However, depending upon the weather conditions, large quantities of the water may have been transpired (evaporated from the leaves), or evaporated from the dish.

Suitable plant materials for testing for water are pieces of apple or potato. It is sufficient merely to sprinkle a little anhydrous copper(II) sulphate on a freshly cut piece of the material.

Experiment 9.8   How much water does plant material contain?

Each group requires:
   plant material, e.g. cabbage, carrot, lettuce, potato, and seeds, as
      required (pea seeds — not dried peas — are suitable)
access to:
   balance (lever-arm type)
   oven set at about 80 °C

It is important, for the sake of making valid comparisons, to take approximately equal amounts of material. However, it may be desirable to take an amount other than 10 g if it seems to be more convenient.
   Most living material contains a high percentage of water. Seeds contain very little and show few signs of life until they are watered.

Q34 There is always a loss in weight, but the amount varies.
Q35 Loss of water.
Q36 No definite answer can be given as it obviously depends upon the material used.
Q37 The seeds (probably).

Experiment 9.9   Can steel float?

Each group requires:
   beaker, 100 cm^3
   teat pipette
   detergent (washing-up liquid)
   steel wool

Q38 It appears to have a very thin 'skin-like' surface. (The answer 'Because the ball of steel wool is very light' may be given but the addition of detergent to the water, which results in the ball sinking, makes it clear that this answer is not satisfactory.)
Q39 It sinks. This is due to the surface 'skin' being broken by the detergent.
Q40 By using the surface 'skin' for support.
Q41 By spraying the surface with something which breaks the surface 'skin' such as a detergent.

Experiment 9.10   Water drops on a waxed surface

Each group requires:
  microscope slide coated with a thin layer of candle wax
  straight pin
  detergent (washing-up liquid)

Experiment 9.11   Making a water turbine

Each group requires:
  cork
  detergent bottle (plastic 'squeezy' bottle)
  knitting needle
  scissors

Pupils themselves will probably be able to provide both detergent
bottles and knitting needles.

Experiment 9.12   Drying blotting paper

Each group requires:
  coloured blotting paper, 15 x 12.5 cm (4 sheets)
  glass plates, at least 15 x 12.5 cm (4)
  scissors
  teat pipette

Q42 In part (a).
Q43. In (a) the paper has the greatest surface area for evaporation.
Q44 It feels cold.
Q45 The smell of acetone (or ether).
Q46 It has evaporated.

Experiment 9.13   The effect of evaporation

Each group requires:
  cottonwool
  length of thread (string)
  retort stands and bosses (2)
  thermometers, −10 to 110 °C (3)
  ether

Q47 The thermometer which has cottonwool soaked in ether.
Q48 The cottonwool should feel cold and dry.
Q49 The thermometer which has dry cottonwool round it, because
there has been little or no evaporation.
Q50 It lowers the temperature.
Q51 As sweat, which is mainly water, evaporates from the surface
of the skin it takes heat energy from the skin, so cooling the body.

Experiment 9.14 Making water climb

Each group requires:
1 *(figure 9.25 of the students' book):*
  beaker, 250 cm³
  set of three capillary tubes of different bore but equal length
  water, coloured with a suitable dye, e.g. eosin (red ink)
2 *(figure 9.26 of the students' book):*
  cork to fit test-tube
  straight pin or drawing pin
  strip of coloured blotting paper, 1 x 11 cm
  test-tube, 150 x 25 mm
3 *(figure 9.27 of the students' book):*
  shallow trough, about 45 x 20 cm
  house bricks (4)
  piece of slate, about 25 x 5 cm, roofing felt, or thick polythene
    sheeting

Results:

1 Water climbs highest in the narrowest tube.
2 A change in the colour of the blotting paper indicates a rise in the water level.
3 Brick A becomes damp but brick B does not as the slate prevents water rising by capillarity.

Q52 Brick A should be wet; brick B should be dry.
Q53 To prevent dampness rising from the ground, by capillarity, up the inside walls of the house.
Q54 Because they were built without a damp-proof course.

Experiment 9.15 What happens to water when it freezes?

Each group requires:
  beaker, 250 cm³
  Bunsen burner
  gauze
  measuring cylinder, say 100 cm³
  ruler, marked in cm
  tripod
  ice cubes (3)

Q55 It is less.
Q56 More.
Q57 It increases.
Q58 The freezing of water causes the burst pipes because of the expansion but they do not appear to be burst until the ice melts.

10 Reproduction

One becomes many

Bacteria dividing. Many film loops are available on bacteria showing the process of fission.

   Q1   128.

Experiments 10.1, 10.2, 10.3, and 10.4 should be set up when convenient. It is not necessary to wait for the results of one before proceeding to the next.

Experiment 10.1   Can a single duckweed become more than one?

Each group requires:
   jam jar
   duckweed *(Lemna)*
   good garden soil

There are several common species of *Lemna.* Two of the most common are found floating on the surface of static water. They are shown in figure 10.1. Either of these is satisfactory for this experiment. The addition of soil, which is likely to contain mineral salts, will help in growth.

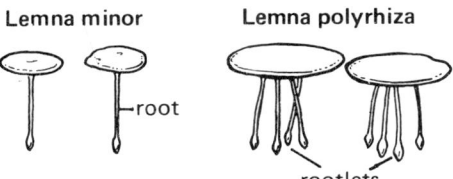

Figure 10.1

Q2 Yes, most should. (The plants divide and new ones are formed.)

Additional experiment using couch grass

The underground shoots of couch grass (figure 10.2) can usefully be used to demonstrate plant reproduction. Some possible investigations are:
1 plant pieces of shoot from between nodes only;
2 plant pieces having several nodes but without axillary buds;
3 plant pieces having several nodes and with at least one axillary bud.

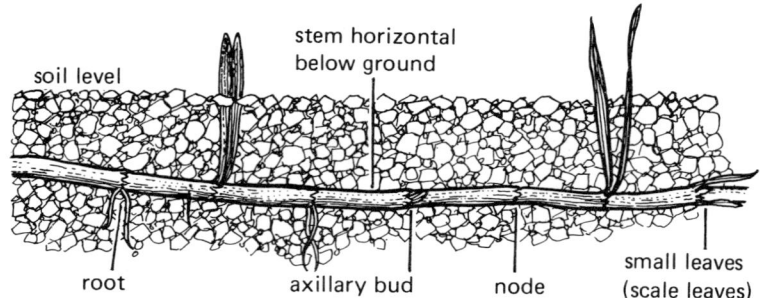

Figure 10.2 The underground shoot of couch grass.

Investigations 1 and 2 are unlikely to result in new plant growth; method 3 should show reproduction.

Experiment 10.2   Can a new plant grow from a piece of the parent plant?

Each group requires:
   plant pot
   polythene bag
   rubber band
   scissors or secateurs
   garden soil
   silver sand
access to:
   geranium plant

The geranium cuttings should be left until new shoots begin to appear.

   Q3 If one is lifted, the roots can be demonstrated, thus showing that a complete plant has been formed. The others can be left undisturbed to provide next year's stock.
   Q4 Yes, most likely.

Experiment 10.3   Can a new plant grow from a piece of root?

Each group requires:
   drawing pins (to fasten polythene)
   polythene sheeting
   scissors
   seed box with soil
   splints for labels

access to:
complete dandelion plants (dock can be used as an alternative)

Small shoots begin to appear in approximately two weeks.

Q5 To cut down water loss from the soil.

Q6 In general, the nearer to the top of the root, the greater is the chance of a new shoot developing.

Experiment 10.4   Can a new plant grow from a piece of leaf?

Each group requires:
seed box with polythene sheet *or* propagating frame
access to:
Begonia rex plant

If a leaf cutting begins to grow, this can be taken as evidence that root formation has begun.

Rooting hormones will help to ensure that a high proportion of the cuttings take. Seradix B and Hortamone A are common ones on the market. The use of a soil propagator is also helpful though not essential.

There are many alternative techniques which may be tried if enough material is available. For example, the entire leaf may be placed on the soil surface and held down by small weights (e.g. pebbles) or pinned down with pins at the edges.

If the leaf cuttings, after they have taken, are carefully removed and potted, next year's stock can be ensured.

Q8 Yes, in some cases.

Vegetative propagation

Q9 Deep-red flowers and about two metres high.

Q10 By dividing the root stock.

Methods of propagation:
layering — carnation
cuttings — blackcurrant
suckers — raspberries
splitting the tuber — dahlia
dividing the root stock — Michaelmas daisy
pegging the runners — strawberry
grafting — apples
from seed potatoes — potatoes

Hydra

Hydra is often difficult to find locally but may be obtained from most biological suppliers. The green *Hydra,* if it can be obtained, is likely to survive longer.

It is best observed by leaving it in a small container for some time and then holding the container up to a light. Favourable conditions are an adequate food supply and warmth.

A useful film loop on feeding and reproduction of *Hydra,* is available.

Experiment 10.5   Looking at Hydra

Each group requires:
    microscope or hand lens
access to:
    prepared slides of budding *Hydra*

Q11 Bud(s) should be visible on the prepared slides.

Experiment 10.6   Looking at herrings

Each group requires:
    hand lens
    microscope slides (2)
    male and female herring roes

Most fishmongers will provide the herring roe, but it is likely to be difficult to obtain at certain times of the year.

Q13 It is about to fertilize the egg.

Q14 Eggs are much larger than sperms, because they contain food for the developing embryo.

Q15 A tail-like structure and a head-like structure.

Q16 To assist in swimming movements.

Q17 It increases the chance of fertilization.

Q18 In spite of shoaling, many eggs will be wasted and not fertilized due to the great volume of water into which they are shed. Only about 0.01 per cent of the eggs fertilized actually grow into fish.

Toads

Q19 The toad is bigger and has a flatter body than the frog which is ideal for concealment. Its eyes are more on top of its head than those of the frog. The hind limbs of the toad are more strongly webbed, and it has three claws in each hind limb.

Q20 It is easier for the female to carry the male.

Q21 Yes, because there is an increased chance of fertilization as the sperms are poured directly over the eggs as they are shed.

Q22 It is most unlikely that they will all hatch. About 10 per cent should do so.

Q23 Not all will have been fertilized.

Q24 Because the sperms are designed to swim in order to fertilize the eggs.

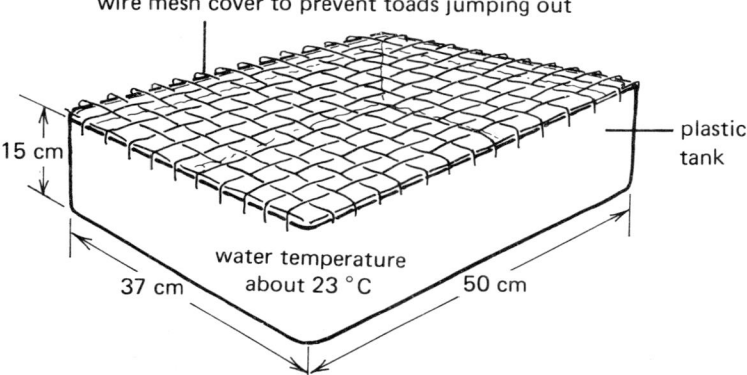

Figure 10.3 A tank for keeping African clawed toads.

Injecting toads with pregnyl to ensure mating

Pregnyl, chorionic gonadotrophin (medical grade), can be obtained from Philip Harris Ltd. It should be kept under lock and key and a written record kept of how it is used. Toads must not be injected in front of the children (Home Office Regulation).

A single injection can be carried out using the following quantities:

male — 100 i.u.
female — 500 i.u.

If the injection is carried out in the late afternoon, the toads should be paired by the following morning. To be certain, at least two pairs should be injected. (See figure 10.4.)

A single injection usually induces mating (amplexus) but, if egg-laying is definitely required a primary injection — male 50 i.u. and female 100 i.u. — followed four days later by a final injection of male 100 i.u. and female 300 i.u. may be needed. A useful film loop, 'African-clawed toad — injection and pairing', is obtainable from Longman in Standard or Super-8 versions.

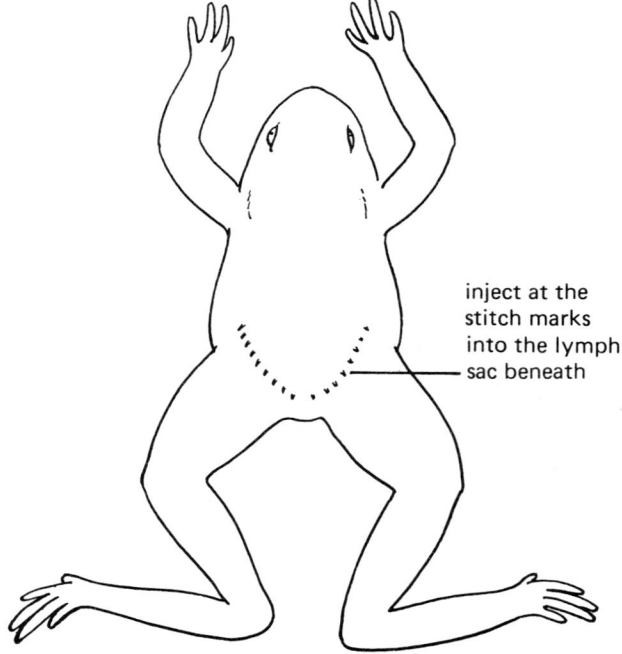

Figure 10.4 Injecting a toad.

Rearing tadpoles

After injecting the adults, a piece of muslin (or a nylon stocking) placed in the tank makes it easy to remove the spawn which tends to collect on it. This spawn should be kept in a tank similar to that shown in figure 10.5. Under these conditions, the spawn takes about eight weeks to develop into small toads.

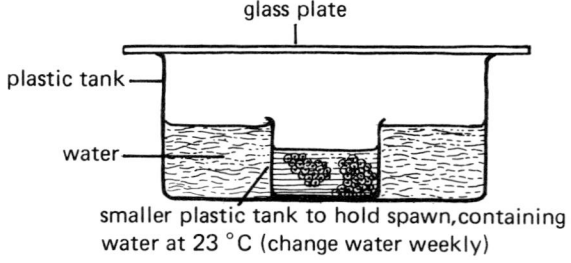

Figure 10.5 A tadpole-rearing tank.

Powdered nettle leaves sprinkled on to the surface of the water provide food for the tadpoles. Excess of this powder should be removed at intervals.

Q25 Siamese fighting fish; heron — neck stretched and erect; many crabs — exaggerated claw movements.

Locusts

A film loop, 'Development of the locust: (1) Pairing and egg laying', is available from Longman in Standard or Super-8 versions.

Q26 No answer can, of course, be given to this.
Q27 So that it is possible for male and female genital openings to meet.
Q28 More likely, because sperms being placed inside the female leads to less waste.
Q29 Protection, especially against drying up which is further assisted by the froth in which they are laid.
Q30 The locust. Some parental care is given in that the female ensures some protection for the eggs.

Other egg-laying animals

Q31 It is important to mention not only the presence of the developing embryo but also that of food.

The animals in the photographs protect their eggs as explained below.

Figure 10.22 The emu is guarding its eggs. The eggs of the emu have hard shells. The father hatches the first brood and the mother the second.
Figure 10.23 The yellow rat snake lays eggs which have a tough rubbery protective shell. It coils itself round the eggs to protect them.
Figure 10.24 Turtle eggs have a hard shell and are buried in the ground.
Figure 10.25 The cockroach lays its eggs in a hard case (egg capsule). This contains sixteen eggs and is deposited in a warm sheltered spot near food.

Q32 There is no need to store food in the egg as the developing embryo obtains food directly from the mother.

Rats

Q33 Because the eggs produced are very small (0.07 mm diameter).
Q34 Internal.
Q35 Eggs can develop inside the mother and thus get food and protection.
Q36 See photograph or dissection. Count the number of embryos. There are thirteen in the photo; some are more easily seen than others.

Q37 The placenta.

Q38 From the mother. The blood of the mother brings food which diffuses into the embryonic blood supply.

Q39 Food passes into the placenta and from there to the embryo via the umbilical cord.

Q40 It supplies food and provides oxygen (from the mother), and anchors the embryo.

Q41 A watery fluid runs out.

Q42 They protect the developing embryo from mechanical shock.

Q43 The walls must be capable of stretching to accommodate the growing embryo.

Human beings

Q44–46 These questions are included to stress the basic structural similarity between the reproductive organs of man and the rat.

Q47 Containing a developing embryo.

Q48 She has a baby to feed in addition to herself.

Q49 By the fluid-filled amniotic sac which acts as a shock absorber.

Q50 This is mechanically the best way as it prevents injury to limbs during birth.

Good parents

Q51 In figures 10.42, 10.43, and 10.45 the mothers (deer, human, and swallow) are feeding their young. In figure 10.44 the kangaroo is carrying its baby in its pouch. The male stickleback in figure 10.46 is driving a snail away from its young in their nest.

Q52 The human baby.

Other things to do

1 Some less common examples:

Animal	Young
deer	fawn
elephant, whale	calf
eel	elver
lion, bear, fox	cub
salmon	parr
swan	cygnet

2 Birds, fish, frogs, snakes, worms, and snails are some examples.

3 Here are a few examples.

(*a*) *Rabbit.* In preparation for birth the mother makes a nest using grass and her own fur in a special excavation in the ground. When the young are born the mother looks after them. She closes up the entrance to the nest with earth each time it is left. They are fed on milk from the mother.

(*b*) *Kangaroo.* The mother's milk-producing glands develop before she gives birth. After birth the mother picks up the helpless infant with her lips and transfers it to a warm pouch. It is attached by the mother to her teat and milk is squirted down its throat periodically.

(*c*) *Pigeon.* Before the young are born a nest is prepared. The young pigeons are fed on a white fluid (pigeon's milk) from the mother, which is formed in the crop. The young pigeon thrusts it beak into the mouth of the mother and the food is pumped from one throat to the other.

(*d*) *Common Stickleback.* Before the young are born the male stickleback builds a nest from weeds stuck together with 'glue' which is produced in the kidneys. Both parents protect the fertilized eggs by remaining on guard outside the nest for as long as one month. They fan a stream of fresh water through the nest and keep the young near to the nest by moving them with their mouths.

11 Growth

Experiment 11.1　Following growth in gerbils (or mice)

Each group requires:
　graph paper
　ruler marked in cm
　suitable nylon bag
access to:
　Butchart balance
　at least four gerbils or mice marked as explained below

Gerbils or mice can be marked for identification purposes by staining near the base of the tail with the following solutions: green — malachite green; red — basic fuchsine; violet — crystal violet. Each dye should be dissolved in a mixture of 20 cm^3 benzyl alcohol, 60 cm^3 methanol, and 20 cm^3 water. The stains are not permanent and may need to be renewed; they are in no way harmful to the animals.

Gerbils need to be at least four weeks old and mice three weeks old to ensure that they can be handled safely.

It is preferable to make recordings of the mass of the animals during the same lesson each week as this avoids the changes of mass which occur within a single day.

The minimum requirement is four animals, ideally of the same sex.

Q6　Tuesday 2 p.m. because of diurnal variation — activity influences weight e.g. increase after meal.
Q7　(*a*) Yes. (*b*) Yes. Though in neither case was the growth as rapid as at the beginning.
Q10　During the first two years. N.B. Note increase at puberty.
Q12　Hair, nails.
Q13　Head (eyes).
Q14　To weigh the individual plants would mean removal from the pot. This would harm the plants. If the plants are weighed in the pot weight loss due to evaporation and transpiration would affect the results.

Experiment 11.2　Looking at the growth of seedlings

Almost any quick growing seedlings may be used. Oat seedlings have proved to be very suitable since the experiment can be speeded up by taking measurements of the coleoptile (leaf sheath) rather than the true leaves. The whole period of growth then takes about ten days.

Advance preparation — A sufficient number of plant pots can be filled with good garden soil, John Innes potting compost, or a mixture of sand and vermiculite. For oat seedlings, this should be done about fourteen days before they are required. By varying the temperature, growth can be encouraged or retarded as required. Soak enough seeds for the whole class in water for about twenty-four hours, allowing for some not germinating, and plant them in 10 cm plant pots (spaced evenly to allow for ease of measurement). The pots should be numbered for identification purposes.

During the experiment the soil should be kept moist by standing the pots in a shallow bath of water periodically.

Q15 Answers may vary. We would expect pupils to take their experimental results.

Q16 Results should be compared with those of Experiment 11.1.

Q17 There would have been more growth for the same length of time; therefore the curve of the graph would be steeper.

It is perhaps surprising that cold conditions should speed up growth 'and development. It is however a well-known practice to give seeds and seedlings a cold treatment for such a purpose (vernalization).

Experiment 11.3   Do all trees grow at the same rate?

Each group requires:
cotton
ruler marked in cm
quantity of suitable twigs from various trees including if possible ash, oak, and sycamore

Q18 Answers will vary.

Q19 By taking a class average.

Q20 Answers will vary but most likely not.

Q21 Most likely not.

Q22 Variations in temperature, rainfall, etc.

Experiment 11.4   Measuring the girth of twigs

Each group requires:
cotton
ruler marked in cm
twigs used in Experiment 11.3

Q25 About eighteen years old.

Q26 The outermost one.

Q27 Not markedly different.

Q28 The width of rings indicates growth rate. Therefore the widest ring indicates the period of greatest growth.

Useful addresses

The following organizations may supply materials and wallcharts.

This list is by no means exhaustive and many more firms and organizations will provide material if asked.

Education Officer, Aluminium Federation, Broadway House, Calthorpe Road, Five Ways, Birmingham B15 1TN.

Timber Research and Development Association Ltd, 26 Store Street, London WC1E 7BS.

Education Officer, Dunlop Co. Ltd, Dunlop House, 25 Ryder Street, London SW1Y 6PX.

Copper Development Association, Orchard House, Mutton Lane, Potters Bar, Herts.

British Steel Federation Training Department, 33 Grosvenor Place, London SW1.

Education and Information Department, Textile Council, Productivity Centre, Fieldon House, Mersey Road, Manchester 20.

McDougall's Cookery Service, Wheatsheaf Mills, London E14.

Film and Education Department, Unilever Ltd, Unilever House, Blackfriars, London EC4P 4BQ.

Public Relations Department, Esso Petroleum Ltd, Esso House, 94-98 Victoria Street, London SW1E 5JW.

Shell International Petroleum Co. Ltd, Shell Centre, London SE1 7NA.

The Lead Development Association, 34 Berkeley Square, London W1X 5DA.

British Oxygen Co. Ltd, Hammersmith House, London W6.

Turner Brothers, Asbestos Co. Ltd, Brook Mill, Rochdale, Lancs.

P56 Negretti & Zambra Ltd ?

Index